Southern Living®

TEXAS BBQ

PLATEFULS OF LEGENDARY LONE STAR FLAVOR

★ ★ ★

Oxmoor House®

©2017 Time Inc. Books

Published by Oxmoor House, an imprint of Time Inc. Books
225 Liberty Street, New York, NY 10281

Senior Editor: Katherine Cobbs
Editor: Meredith L. Butcher
Project Editors: Rebecca Sheehan Caine, Lacie Pinyan
Senior Designer: Liane Burns
Junior Designer: Olivia Pierce
Photographers: Time Inc. Food Studios
Prop Stylists: Time Inc. Food Studios
Food Stylists: Time Inc. Food Studios
Recipe Developers and Testers: Time Inc. Food Studios
Senior Production Manager: Greg A. Amason
Assistant Production Director: Sue Chodakiewicz
Copy Editors: Donna Baldone, Julie Gillis
Proofreader: Rebecca Brennan
Indexer: Carol Roberts
Fellows: Helena Joseph, Hailey Middlebrook, Kyle Grace Mills

ISBN-13: 978-0-8487-5336-8

Library of Congress Control Number: 2016959490

First Edition 2017

Printed in the United States of America

10 9 8 7 6 5 4 3 2 1

We welcome your comments and suggestions about Time Inc. Books.
Please write to us at:
Time Inc. Books
Attention: Book Editors
P.O. Box 62310
Tampa, Florida 33662-2310

Time Inc. Books products may be purchased for business or promotional use. For
information on bulk purchases, please contact Christi Crowley in the Special Sales
Department at (845) 895-9858.

TEXAS BBQ

PLATEFULS OF LEGENDARY LONE STAR FLAVOR

★ ★ ★

CONTENTS

TEXAS BARBECUE'S

identity becomes clearer with every juicy bite. It is proud, audacious, inviting, exacting, traditional, and cutting-edge, all at once. The state itself is a mecca for those with a hankering for an exquisitely crafted brisket, cooked low and slow and dusted with a top-secret-recipe dry rub; or a steaming rack of "dinosaur" ribs, gargantuan enough to feed a small army; or a sizzling skillet of undeniably perfect skirt steak fajitas.

The story of Texas barbecue is as mythic, wild, and vast as the Lone Star State itself. Its roots run deep, spanning continents and generations, all bringing distinct flavors into the mix. And then there are the pitmasters. This league of steely chefs who tend the glowing embers is nothing short of alchemists transmuting nature's raw materials into gold. Their stage—though it may be a rusty old smoker—is a gathering place for the community. After all, a whole roasted hog is meant to be shared, and anyone nearby with a functional sense of smell would be drawn to the tantalizing aroma.

The genesis of Texas barbecue can be traced to the Native American, Caribbean, and Mesoamerican tribes who first cooked meat over open flames beneath a canopy of stars. These indigenous peoples knew how to bring out the best in a slab of meat, which spices would dance on the taste buds, and exactly how to translate smoke into layer upon layer of flavor.

The culinary landscape shifted with the arrival of foreign explorers, conquistadors, and settlers to the New World. With them, the French, Spanish, English, Czech, and German pioneers brought cattle and pigs, new cooking methods and technology, wheat, onions, and peaches.

It was in Texas that everything collided. What was left behind (and what continues to develop decade after decade) was an edible revolution—a melding of cultures you can taste. Folks from the Deep South brought their penchant for pork ribs with thick, sweet sauce and a singular ability to chicken-fry just about anything to East Texas. The Acadians, French Catholics displaced from Canada, met with African-Americans migrating westward and created spicy Cajun dishes, like gumbo with andouille sausage. Along the Gulf of Mexico, coastal Texans took to the sea for their bounty, harvesting the briny oyster beds of Galveston Bay and chasing schools of shrimp from Brownsville through the Gulf Intracoastal Waterway. In Central Texas, where Lockhart is considered the state's barbecue capital, dry rubs supplant sauce and brisket is king. The German and Czech settlers made their home in the hills of West Texas and introduced the state to kolache, bratwurst, and mutton. Tex-Mex cuisine arrived in South Texas, where the state borders Mexico and New Mexico. Here, the Mexican people showed cowhands how to prepare barbacoa, salsa, and corn tortillas.

Today, barbecue is in high demand, and Texas 'cue, with its panoply of techniques, tastes, and traditions, is experiencing a significant boom. Mom-and-pop bbq joints are being rediscovered by budding young pitmasters and curious epicureans.

Barbecue is definitely having its moment in the spotlight, but let's be clear—barbecue's future does not rely on its current popularity. Barbecue, to those who know it best, is a living, breathing organism. It has a language, a family tree, and a culture all its own. It grew up long before any of us were here, and it will continue evolving long after we're gone. Just dig in and be glad you're along for the ride.

ALL THAT GRILLS ★★IS★★ GOLD

Before you start cooking, decide which grill or smoker works best for you.

GAS GRILL

GAS GRILLS

Gas grills maintain consistent heat and are very easy to use; they are especially handy for beginners. Everyone has different needs to consider when buying a gas grill. Every grill is different and some come with more bells and whistles than others. If you like to grill out for the whole neighborhood or have a large household, you'll want to opt for a larger model with 4 to 5 burners. If you're just starting out and like to grill a couple times a week, opt for a smaller version with 3 to 4 burners. Before turning the grill on, make sure that the propane or gas valve is open. Then turn the knob, and—voilà—it's lit. To properly heat the grill, turn all the burners to high, close the lid, and let the grill preheat for 10 to 15 minutes.

CHARCOAL GRILLS

Charcoal grills are less expensive than gas grills. While they are typically more hands-on, these grills have another advantage over gas grills in that they impart a characteristic smoky flavor. If you've got one of these grills, use a chimney starter to help with lighting the coals. It will take about 15 to 30 minutes to get the coals lit, depending on the type of charcoal you use. Once the coals are lit, pour the coals into the bottom of the grill (below the grill grate), replace the grill grate, and close the lid. Be sure that the air vents in the top and bottom are open. To increase the heat of the fire, open the vents wide. To decrease the heat, partially close the vents. Don't close the vents all the way unless you want the fire to go out.

CHARCOAL GRILL   SMOKER

SMOKERS

Water smokers (pictured) are probably the most common type of smoker since they are relatively inexpensive and fairly easy to operate. Most are bullet-shaped and come with a water pan. The water in the water pan acts as a temperature regulator and also often keeps meats that cook for a long period of time more moist. This type of smoker can consistently remain between the 200°F and 250°F range for up to 4 hours, and often longer, depending on what type of coals are used. This equipment creates an indirect cooking environment. The coals and wood are in the bottom section, the water pan in the middle, and the food is in the top where the vents are also located.

Offset smokers (not shown) are also readily available. This design has the charcoal and wood burning off to the side of the main cooking barrel with a vent for lowering or raising the heat. The location of the fuel chamber helps maintain an even temperature for the main cooking barrel. There is also a "baffle" on top to help control the amount of air that comes in, which in turn helps regulate the amount of smoke.

TIP: Resist the temptation to lift the lid during smoking to check meat before the recommended cooking time has elapsed. Doing so allows heat and moisture to escape and adds to the cooking time.

★★ INTO THE WOODS ★★

Another thing that makes authentic Southern barbecue great is the massive amount of flavor you can impart from the type of wood you use in smoking recipes. From peach and apple to mesquite and hickory, there are many different options available.

WOOD CHIPS

For smokers with small baskets, wood chips or small wood chunks are ideal. Be sure to soak them in water for at least 30 minutes so that they don't catch on fire. Wood chips burn for about 20 minutes, and it's easy to add more to a charcoal fire or to a smoker box if they run out before you'd like. Add a handful or two for an additional 10 to 20 minutes of smoke time.

SMOKING BASICS

It is a lot easier to smoke foods than you might think. If you're using a water smoker, the water helps to regulate the heat and also keeps the environment moist, which results in a juicier finished product. Simply pour water into the water pan to the fill line and place it in the smoker. Place soaked chips directly over hot coals and close the lid tightly to smoke. If you're using a gas or charcoal grill to smoke, you can still achieve a delicious result. For gas grills, you'll want to use a smoker box. Place soaked wood chips into the smoker box and close the lid tightly. If you don't have a smoker box, you can make your own by placing soaked chips in a disposable foil pan and covering tightly with heavy-duty aluminum foil. Poke several holes in the foil to allow the smoke to escape. For smoking in a charcoal grill, place soaked chips or chunks directly onto the hot coals and close the grill lid tightly. Add more charcoal, chips, or chunks as needed.

WOOD CHUNKS

For smokers with large fire baskets or chambers, you'll want to use larger wood chunks. These can range in size from as small as golf balls to as big as grapefruits. Wood chunks will burn for about 2 hours when placed over charcoal (they're too large to place in most smoker boxes).

★★ FIRE IT UP ★★

Basically, charcoal is pre-burned wood and is available in two main varieties: charcoal briquettes and lump charcoal. When folks first began grilling, they did so over a wood fire, imparting a wonderful smoky flavor into foods. However, this type of fire creates an incredible amount of smoke and often requires a long wait time for the fire to die down enough to reach the desired temperature. Charcoal was produced to prevent both of these drawbacks.

LUMP CHARCOAL

When wood logs are slowly burned in a pit or kiln, the water and resins are removed to create charcoal. These lumps are easy to light and create a relatively even range of heat. They also emit a flavorful smoke reflective of the type of wood from which they are made. Be sure you know what you're buying though. The bag should tell you what type of wood it is. Look for those with big lumps of charcoal, about the size of an apple.

CHARCOAL BRIQUETTES

This type of charcoal is the most popular in the U.S. because of its low price point and ready availability. These little black nuggets consist of compressed sawdust, coal, and fillers like cornstarch. They create an even, easy-to-predict heat ideal for grilling over a long period of time. But beware: Some briquettes are sold presoaked in lighter fluid to help start more easily. If you're not careful to burn off the lighter fluid completely, it will impart a chemical taste to your food.

HOW TO PREPARE CHARCOAL

STEP 1: Fill bottom of a chimney starter with a few pieces of crumpled newspaper. Pour charcoal over the newspaper (fill entirely for a longer-burning fire). Light the newspaper through the holes in the chimney.

STEP 2: Let the charcoal burn until it is lightly coated with ash. For lump charcoal, it will take about 15 minutes; for briquettes, it will take about 20 to 30 minutes.

STEP 3: Remove the grill grates and pour the lit coals into the bottom of the grill. For direct grilling, spread the coals in an even layer. For indirect grilling, pile them to one side.

STEP 4: To prepare coals without a chimney starter, build a pyramid of coals and light them, starting in the middle. Once lit, pile more coals on top. The fire is ready when all the coals are bright orange and coated with ash. Arrange coals according to step 3.

TIP: When following quick-grilling recipes, if space allows, keep one side of the grill for indirect grilling. That way, if you have a flare-up, you can easily move the food to the cooler side and avoid overcooking or burning.

DIRECT OR INDIRECT

So you've got your grill ready to go. Now what? Well, you'll want to determine if the recipe you're making calls for a direct or an indirect grilling method. Both can be done on either a gas or charcoal grill.

DIRECT HEAT

With direct grilling, food is cooked hot and fast directly over the fire. This method works best with thin and tender cuts of meat like burgers, steaks, vegetables, and fish. Don't try to cook a large roast using this method—the outside of the meat will likely burn before the inside is cooked. For direct grilling using a gas grill, simply turn the knob of the burner to the desired temperature and cook the food directly over the heat source. If using a charcoal grill, spread the lit coals in one even layer on the bottom of the grill.

INDIRECT HEAT

With indirect grilling, food is cooked low and slow beside the fire. Often, the meat is seared first directly over the fire and then moved to the side to finish cooking. Meat can also be cooked solely on the indirect side. This method is ideal for whole chickens, large roasts, and pork shoulders. Many refer to this as "authentic barbecue." For indirect heat using a gas grill, light the burners on one side of the grill and place the meat on the unlit side. If using a charcoal grill, pile the lit coals to one side of the grill, replace the grill grate, and place the food over the unlit side.

★ ★ ★

BEYOND BBQ

Smoky Sides

Where there's smoke there's flavor. Think beyond meats and vegetables on the grill. Dry grains and starches like farro, grits, and rice can take on barbecue flavor too. Simply place the dry grains in a single layer in an aluminum pan. Place the pan, uncovered, on the rack of a grill that has smoking wood chips, or on the rack of a smoker that is smoking generously. Close the lid. Smoke the dry grains for 2 to 5 minutes, then remove and prepare them as usual for your recipe. Say "howdy" to a new favorite side dish.

★★★

CONDIMENTS
rubs, sauces & spreads

★★★

RUBS

Some Texan pitmasters, especially those hailing from Central Texas, refuse to serve barbecue sauce with their perfectly seasoned cuts of meat. Instead, these purists bank on their expertly crafted spice rubs and a tradition of frontier-style preparation.

PORK DRY RUB

Hands-on 5 minutes ★ **Total** 5 minutes ★ **Makes** about 3½ cups

1 cup firmly packed dark brown sugar
1 cup paprika
½ cup granulated garlic
½ cup kosher salt
2 tablespoons dried minced onion
2 tablespoons ground red pepper

2 tablespoons ground chipotle chile pepper
1 tablespoon chili powder
1 tablespoon ground cumin
1 tablespoon freshly ground black pepper
1 tablespoon dry mustard

Stir together all the ingredients. Store in an airtight container up to 1 month.

OLD WEST DRY RUB

Hands-on 8 minutes ★ **Total** 8 minutes ★ **Makes** about ¾ cup

⅓ cup paprika
2 tablespoons granulated sugar
2 tablespoons dark brown sugar
2 teaspoons table salt
2 teaspoons garlic powder

1 teaspoon kosher salt
1 teaspoon ground black pepper
1 teaspoon dry mustard
1 teaspoon onion powder
1 teaspoon ground red pepper

Stir together all the ingredients. Store in an airtight container in a cool, dark place up to 6 months.

SMOKY-SWEET BBQ RUB

Hands-on 5 minutes ★ **Total** 5 minutes ★ **Makes** 1 cup

¼ cup kosher salt
¼ cup firmly packed dark brown sugar
2 tablespoons plus 2 teaspoons smoked paprika
2 tablespoons granulated sugar

2 teaspoons garlic powder
2 teaspoons ground black pepper
1 teaspoon dry mustard
1 teaspoon ground cumin
1 teaspoon ground ginger

Stir together all the ingredients until well blended. Store in an airtight container up to 1 month.

TEXAS MEAT RUB

Hands-on 5 minutes ★ **Total** 5 minutes ★ **Makes** 1⅔ cups

¼ cup table salt
¼ cup ancho chile powder
¼ cup garlic powder
¼ cup onion powder

¼ cup seasoned salt
¼ cup ground black pepper
2 tablespoons paprika

Stir together all the ingredients until well blended. Store in an airtight container up to 1 year.

COWGIRL PORK RUB

Hands-on 5 minutes ★ **Total** 5 minutes ★ **Makes** about ⅓ cup

3 tablespoons granulated garlic
2 tablespoons kosher salt
2 teaspoons light brown sugar
2 teaspoons ground black pepper

½ teaspoon ground oregano
½ teaspoon ground cumin
½ teaspoon ground red pepper

Stir together all the ingredients. Store in an airtight container up to 1 month.

BARBECUE RUB

Hands-on 5 minutes ★ **Total** 5 minutes ★ **Makes** 1 cup

⅓ cup grated piloncillo (or dark
  brown sugar)
2½ tablespoons kosher salt
2½ tablespoons seasoned salt
4 teaspoons garlic powder
4 teaspoons ancho chile powder

2 teaspoons ground black pepper
2 teaspoons chili powder
2 teaspoons Texas Meat Rub
  (recipe above)
¾ teaspoon ground cumin

Stir together all the ingredients until well blended. Store in an airtight container up to 1 month.

BRISKET DRY RUB

Hands-on 5 minutes ★ **Total** 5 minutes ★ **Makes** 1 cup

⅓ cup grated piloncillo (or dark
  brown sugar)
2½ tablespoons kosher salt
2½ tablespoons seasoned salt
4 teaspoons garlic powder

4 teaspoons ancho chile powder
2 teaspoons ground black pepper
2 teaspoons Texas Meat Rub
  (recipe above)
¾ teaspoon ground cumin

Stir together all the ingredients until well blended. Store in an airtight container up to 1 month.

BEEF MARINADE

This marinade infuses beef with the aromatic flavors of rosemary and green onions, while honey helps counter the acidity from the vinegar.

Hands-on 5 minutes ★ **Total** 5 minutes ★ **Makes** ⅔ cup

¼ cup balsamic vinegar
2 tablespoons soy sauce
2 tablespoons honey
2 green onions, thinly sliced

2 teaspoons chopped fresh
   rosemary
1½ teaspoons Dijon mustard

Whisk together all the ingredients until well blended.

SWEET-AND-SPICY MARINADE

When Spanish explorers first discovered and unlocked the powers of Texas' native red pepper in the 16th century, its popularity took on global proportions. Today, the state ranks third in pepper production in the U.S. The piquant flavors in this marinade gradually give way to the milder ingredients the longer it stands, making it a pleasing addition to pork and chicken.

Hands-on 8 minutes ★ **Total** 8 minutes ★ **Makes** 2⅔ cups

1 cup ketchup
⅔ cup firmly packed
   brown sugar
½ cup orange juice
⅓ cup Dijon mustard

1 tablespoon Worcestershire
   sauce
1 tablespoon balsamic vinegar
2 teaspoons dried crushed
   red pepper

Whisk together all the ingredients in a medium saucepan. Bring to a boil, and cook, whisking occasionally, 5 minutes. Cool completely before using as a marinade.

TEXAS BARBECUE SAUCE

Sauce is slathered on barbecue to add flavor and moisture. In the Southern belt of East Texas, a great sauce always accompanies the 'cue. It lends balance to intense smoky flavors and cuts the fattiness of the meat.

Hands-on 10 minutes ★ **Total** 10 minutes ★ **Makes** 3 cups

2 cups ketchup
½ cup apple cider vinegar
½ cup Worcestershire sauce
1 small onion, grated
2 ounces (¼ cup) butter

1 tablespoon seasoned salt
1 tablespoon brown sugar
1½ teaspoons chili powder
1½ teaspoons ground black pepper
1 small bay leaf

Bring all the ingredients to a boil in a large saucepan. Reduce heat, and simmer, stirring occasionally, 10 minutes. Remove and discard the bay leaf from the sauce before serving.

BRISKET RED SAUCE

Red sauce, Texas sauce's less-viscous cousin, creates a powerful flavor when paired with a brisket's deep char. An eager heap of cumin in this recipe contributes to its Tex-Mex flair.

Hands-on 10 minutes ★ **Total** 10 minutes ★ **Makes** 3¼ cups

1½ cups apple cider vinegar
1 cup ketchup
½ cup firmly packed light
    brown sugar
¼ cup Worcestershire sauce
2 tablespoons unsalted butter
1 teaspoon table salt

1½ teaspoons onion powder
1½ teaspoons granulated garlic
1½ teaspoons ground cumin
½ teaspoon freshly ground
    black pepper
½ teaspoon ground red pepper

Whisk together all the ingredients in a medium saucepan. Bring to a boil over high, stirring until the butter melts. Remove from heat; serve warm.

CHOWCHOW

The history of chowchow has been long debated, but everyone can agree that chowchow is irresistible on everything from hamburgers to oyster po'boys.

Hands-on 35 minutes ★ **Total** 4 hours, 5 minutes ★ **Makes** about 3 cups

3 cups chopped cabbage
¾ cup chopped onion
¾ cup chopped green tomatoes
½ cup chopped green bell pepper
½ cup chopped red bell pepper
1 tablespoon pickling salt
¾ cup sugar
½ cup white vinegar

¼ cup water
¾ teaspoon mustard seeds
¼ teaspoon celery seeds
¼ teaspoon ground turmeric
½ teaspoon dried crushed red pepper (optional)
1 jalapeño pepper, seeded and finely chopped (optional)

1. Combine the cabbage, onion, green tomatoes, chopped green and red bell peppers, and pickling salt. Cover and chill 2 to 8 hours.

2. Transfer the mixture to a Dutch oven. Add the sugar, vinegar, ¼ cup water, mustard seeds, celery seeds, turmeric, and, if desired, dried crushed red pepper. Bring to a boil over medium-high; reduce heat to medium, and simmer 3 minutes. Cool to room temperature (about 30 minutes). Stir in the jalapeño pepper, if desired. Cover and chill 1 to 8 hours before serving.

TEXAS SWEET ONIONS-AND-PEACH REFRIGERATOR RELISH

In the Texas Hill Country, peaches begin to ripen at the end of May, but their flavors can be enjoyed year-round thanks to this quick and tasty refrigerator relish.

Hands-on 1 hour, 10 minutes ★ **Total** 3 hours, 25 minutes ★
Makes about 10 (8-ounce) jars

2 cups water
2 cups sugar
2 cups apple cider vinegar
¼ cup gin
2 tablespoons table salt
1 tablespoon mustard seeds
1 teaspoon celery salt

½ teaspoon dried crushed red pepper
4 bay leaves, crushed
3 pounds Vidalia onions, finely chopped
3 pounds fresh peaches, peeled and chopped
4 garlic cloves, thinly sliced

Bring the 2 cups water, sugar, vinegar, gin, salt, mustard seeds, celery salt, dried crushed red pepper, and crushed bay leaves to a boil in a Dutch oven over medium-high. Add the onions, peaches, and garlic; boil, stirring occasionally, 15 minutes. Let the mixture cool completely. Store in airtight containers in refrigerator up to 2 weeks.

PEPPERY TEXAS PICKLES

Served next to a plate of succulent barbecue, these tart and spicy pickles are both crunchy condiment and palate cleanser.

Hands-on 40 minutes ★ **Total** 1 hour, 10 minutes ★
Makes 3 quarts

2½ cups sugar
2 cups apple cider vinegar
¼ cup canning-and-pickling salt
¾ teaspoon celery seeds
¾ teaspoon mustard seeds
½ teaspoon ground turmeric
12 medium cucumbers, cut into ¼-inch slices
1 large Vidalia onion, cut into ⅛-inch slices

1. Cook the first 6 ingredients in a large saucepan over high, stirring occasionally, about 3 minutes or until the mixture is hot and the sugar dissolves. (Do not boil.)

2. Place the cucumbers and onions in a 4-quart airtight plastic container. Pour the hot vinegar mixture over the cucumbers and onions. Cool 30 minutes. Serve immediately, or refrigerate in an airtight container up to 2 weeks.

★★★
BEYOND BBQ

Best Maid Pickles

Searching for real pickle pride? Look no further than Mansfield, Texas. The town was crowned the Pickle Capital of Texas in 2013, but its penchant for pickles really began over 90 years ago thanks to the Dalton family. When Mildred Dalton began selling her homemade mayonnaise at her husband's general store in 1926, it was such a hit that customers clamored for her to make other sandwich fixings. So Mildred started pickling and distributing cucumbers from her garden. Today, Best Maid Pickles harvests more than 30 million pounds of cucumbers a season. The company is still owned and operated by the Dalton family, and its product is the Official Pickle of the Dallas Cowboys.

SALSA

No Tex-Mex feast is complete without tortilla chips and generous portions of fresh salsa to pass around the table (the appetizer is the official snack of the state of Texas, after all). While the most basic salsa recipe—tomatoes, chiles, and spices—is centuries old, the beauty of salsa lies in the subtle (or not-so-subtle) ingredient exchanges each chef chooses that make every batch completely one-of-a-kind.

SALSA FRESCA

Salsa fresca, also salsa cruda, has been the foundation of a multitude of Mexican dishes for centuries. Its vibrant, cool taste is thanks to chilled, fresh ingredients, and it is versatile enough to allow room for experimentation.

Hands-on 10 minutes ★ **Total** 10 minutes ★ **Makes** 4 cups

6 cups coarsely chopped tomatoes
1 teaspoon kosher salt
2 teaspoons fresh lemon juice
½ cup firmly packed fresh
    cilantro leaves, coarsely chopped

1 jalapeño pepper, seeded and
    chopped
1 garlic clove, coarsely chopped
½ cup coarsely chopped red
    onion

Process all the ingredients in a food processer 8 to 10 times or to desired consistency. Cover and chill until ready to serve. Refrigerate in an airtight container up to 3 days.

AVOCADO-MANGO SALSA

A heap of this avocado-mango salsa atop a crisp tortilla chip is a tangy, tropical addition to any Tex-Mex tasting party. Try it on grilled fish or stuffed inside a chicken, pork, or shrimp taco.

Hands-on 25 minutes ★ **Total** 25 minutes ★ **Makes** 7¼ cups

5 cups diced ripe avocado
    (about 4 large)
⅓ cup fresh lime juice
    (about 3 limes)
3 cups diced ripe mango
    (about 3 medium)

¼ cup diced red onion
¼ cup chopped fresh cilantro
1 teaspoon table salt

Combine the avocado and lime juice in a bowl. Stir in the mango and remaining ingredients. Refrigerate in an airtight container up to 3 days.

CRANBERRY SALSA

Move over, boring cranberry sauce. This zesty version of the favorite Thanksgiving condiment is wonderful any time of year. Try it with plantain chips for a change of pace.

Hands-on 10 minutes ★ **Total** 10 minutes ★ **Makes** 4½ cups

1 Granny Smith apple, peeled and cut into 8 wedges
1 cup coarsely chopped red onion
1 medium-size red bell pepper, coarsely chopped
1 jalapeño pepper, coarsely chopped
1 (12-ounce) package fresh or frozen cranberries, thawed

⅓ cup apple juice
¼ cup sugar
¼ cup chopped fresh cilantro
1 tablespoon loosely packed lime zest
Kosher salt
Plantain chips

1. Pulse the first 5 ingredients in a food processor 4 to 6 times or until the mixture is chunky, stopping to scrape sides as needed. Add the apple juice and next 3 ingredients; pulse 3 times or to desired consistency.

2. Transfer the salsa to a serving bowl. Stir in the kosher salt to taste. Cover and chill until ready to serve. Serve with the plantain chips. Refrigerate in an airtight container up to 2 days.

TOMATILLO SALSA

The tomatillo, or Mexican husk tomato, is vital for developing the pleasant tartness and green color of this salsa. In Mexico, the popular and delectable sauce is better known as salsa verde.

Hands-on 10 minutes ★ **Total** 45 minutes ★ **Makes** 4 cups

3 pounds fresh tomatillos, husks removed
2 jalapeño peppers, stemmed
1 tablespoon fresh lime juice

4 garlic cloves
2½ cups loosely packed cilantro
1 teaspoon kosher salt

1. Combine the tomatillos, peppers, and water to cover in a Dutch oven. Bring to a boil over medium-high; reduce heat, and simmer 10 minutes or until the tomatillos are tender. Remove from heat; let stand 15 minutes. Drain. Wipe Dutch oven clean.

2. Process the tomatillos, peppers, lime juice, and garlic in a blender until coarsely chopped. Add the cilantro; process until smooth. Return to Dutch oven, and simmer over medium, stirring occasionally, 10 minutes or until thickened slightly.

3. Remove from heat; stir in the salt. Serve at room temperature, or cover and chill until ready to serve. Refrigerate in an airtight container up to 3 days.

Ninfa's on Navigation

Houston

◇◇◇◇◇◇◇◇◇

In Houston, Ninfa "Mama" Laurenzo is credited with inventing the modern fajita platter and inspiring an entire nation to embrace Tex-Mex food in the form of flat beef strips delivered on a sizzling iron comal. The authentically Tex-Mex locale is also famous for its heavenly tomatillo-avocado green sauce that has patrons dipping tortilla chip after tortilla chip into bottomless bowls.

---

*2704 Navigation Blvd
Houston, TX 77003
713-228-1175
ninfas.com*

"NINFA'S" GREEN SAUCE

In 1973, Ninfa Rodriguez Laurenzo was a single mother raising five children in Houston when the idea to open a taco stand appeared to her in a dream. She opened the 10-table Original Ninfa's on Navigation in front of her struggling tortilla factory. The business took off, and "Mama Ninfa" became a legendary entrepreneur and restaurateur. Graciously, the restaurant has shared Ninfa's secret green sauce recipe in the Houston Chronicle. *A variation of the recipe is printed below.*

Hands-on 25 minutes ★ **Total** 50 minutes ★
Makes 6½ cups

5 fresh tomatillos, husks removed
3 medium-size green tomatoes, chopped
2 jalapeño peppers, seeded and chopped
2 large garlic cloves, coarsely chopped
3 medium-size ripe avocados, halved
½ cup coarsely chopped fresh cilantro
2 teaspoons table salt
1 cup sour cream
1 tablespoon fresh lime juice
Tortilla chips

1. Chop the tomatillos. Combine the tomatillos and next 3 ingredients in a medium saucepan. Bring to a boil; cover, reduce heat to medium-low, and simmer 12 minutes. Remove from heat, and cool slightly.

2. Process tomatillo mixture, avocados, and next 2 ingredients in a blender or food processor until smooth, stopping to scrape down sides as needed. Transfer to a serving bowl. Stir in the sour cream and lime juice. Serve warm or chilled with the tortilla chips. Refrigerate in an airtight container up to 3 days.

ROASTED TOMATO AND ANCHO SALSA

The ancho, which is simply a dried poblano pepper, and the roasted vegetables add a smoky dynamic to this traditional salsa.

Hands-on 15 minutes ★ **Total** 2 hours, 50 minutes ★ **Makes** 2½ cups

1 dried ancho chile pepper
5 plum tomatoes, halved
    lengthwise
1 medium onion, quartered
1 large jalapeño pepper, halved
    and seeded

2 garlic cloves
3 tablespoons fresh lime juice
1 teaspoon kosher salt

1. Preheat the oven to 450°F. Lightly grease an aluminum foil-lined jelly-roll pan. Pour boiling water over the ancho chile in a bowl or liquid measuring cup; let stand 20 minutes or until tender. Drain. Remove and discard stem and seeds.

2. Arrange the tomatoes, onion, and jalapeño, cut sides down, in a single layer on prepared jelly-roll pan; sprinkle with the garlic. Bake at 450°F for 30 minutes or until the vegetables are tender; increase oven temperature to broil, and broil 5 minutes or until the vegetables are blistered.

3. Pulse the roasted vegetables in a food processor 6 to 8 times until mixture is chunky. Stop and scrape sides as necessary. Add the ancho chile pepper to food processor; pulse to desired consistency. Stir in the lime juice and salt. Chill in an airtight container up to 3 days.

PICO DE GALLO

This Mexican salsa is about as fresh as it gets. Made with lime juice instead of salsa fresca's lemon juice, pico de gallo's bright flavors are enticing.

Hands-on 10 minutes ★ **Total** 10 minutes ★ **Makes** 3½ cups

3½ cups diced tomato
1 cup finely chopped red onion
¼ cup loosely packed fresh
    cilantro, chopped

3 tablespoons fresh lime juice
½ teaspoon kosher salt
1 jalapeño pepper, minced

Stir together all the ingredients in a bowl; toss gently to combine. Refrigerate in an airtight container up to 3 days.

Fonda San Miguel

Austin

◇◇◇◇◇◇◇◇

The second you walk across the threshold of the heavy carved wooden doors, your senses are sent to a rustic old-world estate somewhere in the Mexican countryside. It's a sensation the restaurant has cultivated since its inception in 1975. And the food is just as transformative. Chargrilled Pollo con Mole is tender and juicy and is bathed in a heavenly mole sauce. Ceviche is fresh and brightly flavorful, and margaritas are handcrafted and not-too-sweet. But the best dish of the house is the Carne Asada a la Tampiqueña with tender, marinated strips of grilled beef tenderloin, a cheese enchilada with mole sauce, and fresh guacamole.

2330 W. North Loop Blvd
Austin, TX 78756
512-459-4121
fondasanmiguel.com

GUACAMOLE

When the Aztecs invented this avocado-based salsa, little did they realize what an impact it would have on modern epicureans. Spaniard conquistadors carried the "alligator pear" back to Europe, where the smooth pulp was spread over toast and topped with a variety of spices. Tortilla chips may be the preferred vehicle for getting this creamy concoction to mouth, but it's equally delicious served with cut veggies.

Hands-on 9 minutes ★ **Total** 9 minutes ★ **Serves** 4

¼ cup finely chopped red onion
¼ teaspoon kosher salt
2 ripe avocados, peeled and chopped
    (about 1½ cups)
½ cup chopped plum tomato (1 large)
1 tablespoon fresh lime juice
Bell pepper strips (optional)

Place the onion, salt, and avocado in a medium bowl; mash with the back of a wooden spoon. Stir in the tomato. Add the lime juice, stirring until the avocado just begins to lose its shape but is still very chunky. Serve with bell pepper strips, if desired.

TEXAS' ONLY ALL-MALT BEER!
DRINK
SHINER
BEER
K. Spoetzl Brewery
PABST
DRINK
GRAND PRIZE
BEER

BLACK BEAN DIP

Bean dips and refried beans are a regular feature of Tex-Mex dinner platters. Serve this as a dip with baked tortilla chips, over scrambled eggs with salsa, or on quesadillas for a fun twist.

Hands-on 16 minutes ★ **Total** 16 minutes ★ **Serves** 12

1 tablespoon olive oil
1½ cups diced onion
2 teaspoons chili powder
1 teaspoon ground cumin
2 tablespoons fresh lime juice
1 tablespoon water
1 teaspoon chopped fresh oregano
½ teaspoon chopped chipotle chile,
    canned in adobo sauce

¼ teaspoon salt
2 (15-ounce) cans black beans, rinsed
    and drained
2 tablespoons crumbled queso fresco
1 tablespoon minced red onion
Chopped fresh cilantro (optional)
60 corn chips

Heat a large nonstick skillet over medium-high. Add oil; swirl to coat. Add onion; sauté 5 minutes or until tender, stirring occasionally. Add chili powder and cumin; sauté 1 minute. Place onion mixture, lime juice, and next 5 ingredients (through black beans) in a food processor; process until smooth. Spoon mixture into a serving bowl; top with queso fresco, red onion, and, if desired, chopped cilantro. Serve with corn chips.

JACK ALLEN'S PIMIENTO CHEESE

Jack Allen's Kitchen, one of Austin's top brunch spots, serves their locally sourced pimiento cheese many ways—with flatbread crackers, blended into potatoes au gratin, and dished into chilled Mason jars.

Hands-on 15 minutes ★ **Total** 15 minutes ★ **Makes** 2 cups

4 ounces cream cheese, softened
¼ cup mayonnaise
1 teaspoon Worcestershire sauce
½ teaspoon sherry vinegar
1 cup (4 ounces) shredded pepper
   Jack cheese
1 cup (4 ounces) shredded extra-
   sharp Cheddar cheese

1 tablespoon grated onion
¼ teaspoon kosher salt
Freshly ground black pepper
½ (12-ounce) jar roasted red
   peppers, drained and finely
   chopped*

Beat the first 4 ingredients at medium speed with an electric mixer until smooth. Stir in remaining ingredients. Cover and chill until ready to serve. Refrigerate in an airtight container up to 1 week.

*To roast fresh red bell peppers, preheat the oven to broil. Line a baking sheet with aluminum foil. Arrange the peppers on prepared baking sheet, and broil 5 inches from heat 5 to 10 minutes on each side or until the bell peppers look blistered. Transfer the bell peppers to a zip-top plastic bag; seal and let stand 10 minutes to loosen skins. Peel, remove and discard seeds, and finely chop.

DEVILED EGGS

Deviled eggs are a must-have hors d'oeuvre for a Southern spread. In the 1800s, the term "deviled" became a popular descriptor for any recipe spicy enough that el diablo himself would be anxious to nibble.

Hands-on 12 minutes ★ **Total** 27 minutes ★ **Serves** 6

6 large eggs
3 tablespoons canola mayonnaise
2 teaspoons Dijon mustard
½ teaspoon fresh lemon juice

¼ teaspoon freshly ground black pepper
2 teaspoons coarsely chopped
   fresh chives
⅛ teaspoon hot paprika

1. Place the eggs in a large saucepan. Cover with water to 1 inch above the eggs; bring just to a boil. Remove from heat; cover and let stand 15 minutes. Drain and rinse with cold running water until cool.

2. Peel the eggs; cut in half lengthwise, and remove yolks. Place the yolks in a bowl; mash with a fork. Stir in the mayonnaise and next 3 ingredients.

3. Spoon the yolk mixture evenly into the egg white halves. Sprinkle with the chives and paprika.

RAJAS CON QUESO

Popular in South Texas, rajas (Spanish for "slices") are strips of poblano peppers typically served with cream during taquizas—taco parties. In this dip, Tex meets Mex with a blend of cheeses and sour cream, which tempers the often unpredictable heat of the poblanos.

Hands-on 35 minutes ★ **Total** 45 minutes ★ **Makes** 3½ cups

2 pounds poblano peppers
1 cup thinly sliced white
    onion
1 garlic clove, minced
Pinch of table salt
2 teaspoons vegetable or
    corn oil
¾ cup milk
1 tablespoon cornstarch
3 tablespoons crema or sour
    cream

1½ cups (6 ounces) shredded
    Monterey Jack or
    quesadilla cheese
1 cup (4 ounces) shredded
    deli white American
    cheese
Table salt and ground black
    pepper
Tortilla chips

1. Preheat the broiler. Line a baking sheet with aluminum foil. Broil the peppers on prepared baking sheet 5 inches from heat 12 to 15 minutes or until the peppers look blistered.

2. Place the peppers in a large zip-top plastic freezer bag; seal and let stand 10 to 15 minutes to loosen skins. Peel the peppers; remove and discard the seeds. Cut the peppers into strips.

3. Sauté the onion, garlic, and salt in hot oil in a medium skillet over medium 8 minutes or until tender. Stir in the pepper strips.

4. Combine the milk and cornstarch in a small bowl, stirring until smooth. Add the milk mixture to skillet. Bring to a light boil. Remove from heat; add the crema and cheeses, stirring until cheese is melted and mixture is creamy. Add the salt and pepper to taste. Serve immediately with the tortilla chips.

★★★
LONE STAR LEGENDS

La Fonda on Main
San Antonio

◇◇◇◇◇◇◇◇

A little more polished than your average Tex-Mex joint, La Fonda's reputation was built on its warm and adept service, elegant setting, and well-appointed menu of Mexican classics. Since its inception in 1930, it is the place locals like to bring out-of-towners—and for good reason. Classic Fish Veracruzana is a staple dish, as are the Tacos de Pato. Located in a beautiful Spanish-style villa near downtown, La Fonda is a taste of Old San Antonio at its best.

*2415 North Main Ave
San Antonio, TX 78212
210-733-0621
lafondaonmain.com*

TEXAS CAVIAR

When New Yorker Helen Corbitt first arrived in Austin in 1940, she almost packed her bags and headed straight back to the Big Apple. The newly hired University of Texas catering professor was tasked with creating an elegant dinner with (at that time) decidedly Texan ingredients, including the unassuming black-eyed pea. In a fit of brilliance, Corbitt concocted Texas Caviar, and it was a hit. Corbitt's ingenuity won her a lifetime of culinary success and recognition as "Tastemaker of the Century" by Texas Monthly. And, yes, she ended up falling in love with Texas, where she became Director of Food Service at Neiman Marcus and went on to live happily ever after.

Hands-on 15 minutes ★ **Total** 15 minutes, plus 8 hours chilling time ★
Makes 7 to 8 cups

2 (15½-ounce) cans black-eyed peas, drained and rinsed
2 plum tomatoes, diced
2 green onions, chopped
1 cup fresh corn kernels (2 ears)*

½ cup chopped red bell pepper
½ cup Salsa Fresca (page 32)
¼ cup chopped fresh cilantro
2 garlic cloves, minced
1 teaspoon table salt

Stir together all the ingredients in a serving bowl. Cover and chill, stirring occasionally, 8 hours.

*1 (8-ounce) can whole kernel corn, drained, may be substituted for fresh corn kernels.

THE ORIGINAL NACHO

In 1943, a few American military wives crossed the Rio Grande from Eagle Pass, Texas, and arrived at the dining room of the Victory Club in Piedras Negras, Mexico. After they settled in with some cocktails, they asked their waiter, Ignacio "Nacho" Anaya, for a new type of snack. The resourceful Anaya topped crisp triangles of fried tortillas with cheese, beans, and jalapeños, named the dainty appetizer after himself, and became an international sensation nearly overnight as his new recipe spread like prairie fire.

Hands-on 5 minutes ★ **Total** 15 minutes ★ **Serves** 4

20 tortilla chips
5 sharp Cheddar cheese
   slices, quartered into
   squares

40 pickled sliced jalapeños
1 (16-ounce) can refried
   beans (optional)
Fresh cilantro

1. Preheat the oven to 400°F.

2. Arrange the tortilla chips in a single layer on a large baking sheet. Top each chip with 1 cheese square and 2 jalapeño slices. Top with 1 tablespoon refried beans, if desired.

3. Bake at 400°F for 5 to 10 minutes or until the cheese melts and edges of chips are browned. Top with cilantro. Serve immediately.

★ ★ ★
BEYOND BBQ

For the Love of Texas

On March 2, 1836, fifty-nine Texan delegates gathered at Washington-on-the-Brazos to declare independence from Mexico and establish the Republic of Texas. Many proud Texans celebrate the signing of the Texas Declaration of Independence with an annual visit to the historic site. Those more far-flung who still have the Lone Star State in their hearts can acknowledge the holiday by throwing a shindig with decidedly Texan food and fun. Serve ice-cold Shiner Premium beer, Dr Pepper, Texas caviar, and Frito pie with Blue Bell ice cream for dessert.

COLESLAW BRISKET SHOOTERS

This clever recipe stars Texas' reigning style of barbecued beef—the brisket—in miniature, perfect for whetting appetites for the main course.

Hands-on 50 minutes ★ **Total** 50 minutes, including slaw ★ **Serves** 12

2 cups milk
2 cups water
1 cup uncooked regular grits
½ teaspoon table salt
1 cup (4 ounces) shredded smoked
    Gouda cheese
½ cup shredded Parmesan cheese

1½ pounds shredded Texas
    Smoked Brisket (without
    sauce) (page 61)
Coleslaw (recipe below)
Barbecue sauce
Garnish: fresh cilantro leaves

1. Bring the milk and 2 cups water to a boil in a saucepan over medium, stirring occasionally. Gradually whisk in the grits and salt; return to a boil. Cover, reduce heat to low, and simmer, stirring occasionally, 10 to 15 minutes or until thickened. Remove from heat; stir in the cheeses until blended.

2. Layer the Texas Smoked Brisket, grits, and Coleslaw in 12 (8-ounce) glasses; drizzle with the barbecue sauce. Serve immediately.

COLESLAW

Creamy, crunchy coleslaw (or sometimes just "slaw") is standard fare at just about any Southern-style gathering, particularly barbecues, picnics, and Fourth of July get-togethers.

Hands-on 10 minutes ★ **Total** 10 minutes ★ **Makes** about 4 cups

⅓ cup mayonnaise
2 tablespoons minced green onions
1 tablespoon sugar
2 tablespoons fresh lemon juice
¼ teaspoon table salt

¼ teaspoon freshly ground
    black pepper
1 (16-ounce) package shredded
    coleslaw mix

Whisk together the first 6 ingredients in a large bowl. Add the coleslaw mix, and toss to coat.

SPICY GRILLED WINGS

Serve these satisfyingly spicy wings paired with the creamy Blue Cheese Sauce and a selection of locally brewed IPAs.

Hands-on 1 hour ★ **Total** 1 hour, 10 minutes, including sauce ★ **Serves** 12

2 teaspoons ground chipotle
   chile pepper
2 teaspoons black pepper
2 teaspoons table salt
4½ to 5 pounds chicken wings
1 tablespoon olive oil
1½ ounces (3 tablespoons) butter
½ cup chopped onion

2 garlic cloves, pressed
1 cup apple cider vinegar
1 (8-ounce) can tomato sauce
1 (6-ounce) can tomato paste
2 tablespoons light brown sugar
2 tablespoons Worcestershire sauce
2 teaspoons hot sauce
Blue Cheese Sauce (recipe below)

1. Light 1 side of grill, heating to 350° to 400°F (medium-high). Combine the first 2 ingredients and 1 teaspoon of the salt. Cut off the chicken wing tips, and discard; cut wings in half at joint. Toss the wings with oil. Sprinkle the chicken with pepper mixture, and toss. Arrange the wings over the unlit side of grill. Grill, covered with grill lid, 18 to 20 minutes on each side or until done.

2. Meanwhile, melt the butter in a saucepan over medium-high; add the onion and garlic, and sauté 5 minutes or until tender. Reduce heat to medium. Add the vinegar, next 5 ingredients, and remaining 1 teaspoon salt. Cook, stirring occasionally, 10 to 12 minutes or until bubbly.

3. Transfer the wings to a clean bowl; add half of the butter mixture, reserving remaining mixture. Toss the wings gently to coat. Place the wings on the lit side of grill. Grill, covered with grill lid, 10 minutes or until browned, turning occasionally. Toss the wings with reserved butter mixture. Serve with the Blue Cheese Sauce.

BLUE CHEESE SAUCE

Experiment with the flavors of this recipe by using Texas blue cheese such as Bosque Blue or Mozzarella Company Deep Ellum Blue.

Hands-on 10 minutes ★ **Total** 10 minutes ★ **Makes** about 2 cups

1 (8-ounce) container sour cream
⅓ cup buttermilk
1 (4-ounce) wedge blue cheese,
   crumbled
2 tablespoons chopped fresh chives

1 teaspoon lemon zest
1 tablespoon fresh lemon juice
1 teaspoon coarse-grained mustard
½ teaspoon table salt
¼ teaspoon black pepper

Stir together all the ingredients until well blended. Cover and chill until ready to serve.

BACON-WRAPPED DOVE POPPERS

Dove hunting has been a veritable institution in Texas as long as people have graced the land. In 1895, an anonymous writer wrote in the San Antonio Light *of the petite game bird, "They delight the hunter's heart with their simple but melodious song." These days, dove season begins on September 1, and successful huntsmen have invented abundant recipes for serving their quarry. If you don't have dove around, use chunks of pork or boneless chicken thigh as a substitute in this recipe. You may cut the bacon slices in half if you prefer.*

Hands-on 35 minutes ★ **Total** 55 minutes, including rub ★ **Serves** 8 to 10

30 skinned and boned dove breasts
Texas Meat Rub (page 21)
1 (8-ounce) package cream cheese,
    softened

4 jalapeño peppers, seeded
    and cut into 30 thin strips*
2 (16-ounce) packages bacon slices
Wooden picks

1. Preheat the grill to 350° to 400°F (medium-high). Sprinkle the dove with Texas Meat Rub. Spoon 2 teaspoons of the cream cheese, and place 1 jalapeño strip on 1 side of each dove breast, leaving a ¼-inch border. Roll up, starting at 1 short side. Wrap each stuffed jalapeño with 1 bacon slice; secure with wooden picks.

2. Grill the dove, without grill lid, 6 minutes on each side or until bacon is crisp and dove is done.

Serrano peppers or red Fresno peppers may be substituted for jalapeño peppers.

LAND & SEA

beef, pork, chicken, fish & shellfish

TEXAS SMOKED BRISKET

In Texas, pulled pork barbecue has its place, but smoked brisket cooked low and slow is king. Dolled up with a dry rub, soaked in sauce, or left au naturel, this generous cut of beef first showed up on deli counter menus in El Paso in 1910.

Hands-on 35 minutes ★ **Total** 7 hours, 5 minutes, including rub and sauce ★ **Serves** 12 to 14

Wood chips
½ cup Brisket Dry Rub
   (page 21)

1 (6½-pound) flat-cut brisket
Brisket Red Sauce (page 24)

1. Soak wood chips in water 30 minutes. Prepare the smoker according to manufacturer's directions, bringing internal temperature to 225° to 250°F; maintain temperature for 15 to 20 minutes. Sprinkle the Brisket Dry Rub on brisket, pressing gently to adhere. Let the brisket stand 10 minutes. Drain the wood chips, and place on the coals. Place the brisket on the upper cooking grate; cover with smoker lid.

2. Smoke the brisket, maintaining temperature inside the smoker between 225° and 250°F, for 5½ to 6 hours or until a meat thermometer inserted into thickest portion of brisket registers between 195° and 205°F. Add additional charcoal and wood chips as needed. Remove the brisket from smoker, and let stand 10 minutes. Cut the brisket across the grain into thin slices, and serve with the Brisket Red Sauce.

★ ★ ★
LONE STAR LEGENDS

Stanley's Bar-B-Q
Tyler

◇◇◇◇◇◇◇◇◇

This low-key locale is everything you'd want in a barbecue joint with its informal setting and weekends of live music. Here, brisket is tender and juicy, and the ribs are some of the best around. Peppery smoked turkey is also a house favorite, as is the classic chopped brisket sandwich and the "Ex-Wife" sandwich, made of a combo of pulled pork and sliced brisket.

*525 S. Beckham Ave
Tyler, TX 75702
903-593-0311
stanleysfamous.com*

BEEF RIBS WITH SORGHUM GLAZE

Benjamin Franklin is credited with the first written record of sorghum, then known as broomcorn and later as milo, in the United States in 1757. This thick sorghum glaze gives barbecued ribs a kiss of sweetness with more flavor complexity than honey or cane syrup.

Hands-on 45 minutes ★ **Total** 6 hours, 25 minutes, plus 12 hours chilling time ★ **Serves** 8

4 (2½-pound) racks beef rib-back ribs (center cut)
¼ cup sugar
¼ cup kosher salt
2 tablespoons freshly ground black pepper
1 teaspoon garlic powder
1 teaspoon onion powder
1 teaspoon smoked paprika
½ teaspoon ground red pepper
1 cup sorghum syrup
1 cup apple cider vinegar
1 tablespoon coarsely ground black pepper
4 cups wood chips

1. Rinse and pat the ribs dry. If desired, remove the thin membrane from back of the ribs by slicing into it and pulling it off. (This will make the ribs more tender.) Combine the sugar and next 6 ingredients. Massage the sugar mixture into the meat, covering all sides. Wrap the ribs tightly with plastic wrap, and place in zip-top plastic freezer bags; seal and chill 12 hours.

2. Whisk together the sorghum and next 2 ingredients in a saucepan over medium-high. Bring to a boil, stirring occasionally; reduce heat to medium, and cook, stirring occasionally, 6 minutes or until the mixture is reduced by half. Cool completely.

3. Soak chips in water 30 minutes. Light 1 side of grill, heating to 250° to 300°F (low); leave other side unlit. Spread wood chips on a large sheet of heavy-duty aluminum foil; fold edges to seal. Poke several holes in top of the pouch with a fork. Place the pouch directly on lit side of grill; cover with grill lid.

4. Place the ribs over unlit side, and grill, covered with grill lid, 2 hours. Turn the rib slabs over; grill 2 hours or until tender. Cook the ribs 30 more minutes, basting frequently with sorghum mixture.

5. Remove the ribs from grill, and let stand 10 minutes. Cut the ribs, slicing between bones.

★ ★ ★
LONE STAR LEGENDS

Florida's Kitchen

Livingston

◇◇◇◇◇◇◇◇◇

For a down-home country experience in a no-frills, laid-back environment, Florida's Kitchen is the place. It may not look like much from the outside, but once you're seated in front of a plate of family style good cooking from owners Sly and Ms. Florida Harris, it won't matter a pinch. The barbecue ribs are tender and juicy and glazed in a sweet and tangy sauce, while the catfish is golden and crispy. The key is to get there early, as ribs tend to sell out later in the day.

796 FM 350 S
Livingston, TX 77351
866-9721-6078
floridaskitchen.com

SMOKED BEEF TENDERLOIN

One of the leanest and most tender cuts of beef gets the Texas treatment when left to the magic of the smoker. Mellow and fruity applewood smoke laces the meat with subtle sweetness while the ancho chile and garlic powders coax the savory beef flavor into the spotlight.

Hands-on 20 minutes ★ **Total** 3 hours, 10 minutes, including rub ★
Serves 12 to 16

¼ cup firmly packed light brown
   sugar
¼ cup seasoned salt
2 tablespoons kosher salt
3 tablespoons Texas Meat Rub
   (page 21)

2 tablespoons garlic powder
2 tablespoons ancho chile powder
2 tablespoons cracked black pepper
1 (7- to 8-pound) beef tenderloin,
   trimmed
3 applewood chunks

1. Stir together the first 7 ingredients; rub 1 cup of the brown sugar mixture over the tenderloin. Reserve remaining brown sugar mixture for another use. Cover the tenderloin, and let stand at room temperature for 1 hour.

2. Meanwhile, soak the wood chunks in water 30 minutes. Prepare the smoker according to manufacturer's directions, bringing internal temperature to 225° to 250°F; maintain temperature for 15 to 20 minutes.

3. Drain the wood chunks, and place on hot coals. Cover with smoker lid, and let stand 5 minutes or until the wood chunks begin to smoke. Place the tenderloin on cooking grate; cover with smoker lid.

4. Smoke the tenderloin, maintaining temperature inside smoker between 225° and 250°F for 1 hour and 15 minutes or until a meat thermometer inserted into thickest portion registers 135°F or to desired degree of doneness.

5. Remove from grill. Cover loosely with aluminum foil, and let stand 15 minutes. Cut across the grain into thin slices.

Onions

Texas grows more sweet onions than any other vegetable crop. In 1898, settlers sprinkled Bermuda onion seeds near the South Texas town of Cotulla, and by 1904 there were more than 500 acres of the Caribbean transplant in South Texas. By 1920, Texas was out-producing the Bermuda islands. The primary onions produced and exported over the better part of the following century were from Texas, including the hybrid Granex, which was planted in many other states under different names such as the well-known Georgia Vidalia.

ARRACHERA WITH ANCHO AND PASILLA ADOBO

Adobo is a sauce or paste made with a spicy blend of chiles and herbs used in the traditional cuisine of Spain, Peru, Mexico, and Portugal. An international favorite, it is no surprise that variations of adobo abound.

Hands-on 50 minutes ★ **Total** 3 hours, 25 minutes, including adobo and roasted garlic ★ **Serves** 6

4 pounds flank or skirt steak
½ teaspoon table salt
¼ cup vegetable oil
1 onion, diced
10 garlic cloves, minced
Ancho and Pasilla Adobo
   (recipe opposite)

1½ teaspoons whole cumin
   seeds, toasted and ground
2 cups tomato puree
2 cups water

1. Sprinkle the steak with salt. Brown, in batches, 3 to 4 minutes on each side in hot oil in a large Dutch oven over medium-high. Remove the steak, reserving the drippings in Dutch oven.

2. Sauté the onion and garlic in hot drippings 5 minutes. Add the Ancho and Pasilla Adobo, cumin, tomato puree, steak, and any accumulated juices from steak to Dutch oven.

3. Bring to a light boil. Add the 2 cups water and salt to taste. Cover, reduce heat to low, and simmer 2 hours or until the meat is tender. Remove the steak from Dutch oven, and let stand 15 minutes. Cut the steak diagonally across the grain into thin slices.

4. Meanwhile, cook the sauce, uncovered, 15 minutes or until thickened. Serve with the steak.

ANCHO AND PASILLA ADOBO

Hands-on 20 minutes ★ **Total** 30 minutes ★ **Makes** 3½ cups

8 dried ancho chile peppers
10 dried pasilla peppers
1½ teaspoons whole cumin seeds
1½ teaspoons dried Mexican
    oregano

1 cup fresh orange juice
½ cup fresh lime juice
⅓ cup firmly packed brown sugar
2 tablespoons pureed roasted
    garlic*

1. Preheat the oven to 350°F. Place the ancho chile and pasilla peppers on a baking sheet. Bake at 350°F for 5 minutes. Remove from oven. Pour boiling water to cover the peppers in a bowl; let stand 5 minutes or until tender. Drain, reserving water. Discard the stems and seeds.

2. Place a small skillet over medium-high until hot; add the cumin seeds and oregano, and cook, stirring constantly, 1 minute or until toasted. Remove from heat.

3. Place the cumin and oregano in a mortar bowl or spice grinder; grind using a pestle or grinder until mixture becomes a medium-fine powder.

4. Process the peppers, spice mixture, orange juice, lime juice, brown sugar, roasted garlic, and ½ cup of the reserved water in a blender until smooth, stopping to scrape down sides as needed. Add salt to taste.

*To roast fresh garlic, preheat the oven to 425°F. Cut off pointed end of the garlic bulb; place the garlic on a piece of aluminum foil, and fold foil to seal. Bake at 425°F for 30 minutes; cool 10 minutes. Squeeze pulp from garlic cloves. Makes about 1 tablespoon paste (about 15 cloves)

ADOBO GRILLED BEEF RIB-EYES

In the U.S., the term rib-eye technically refers to a boneless steak, but grill up an extra-flavorful bone-in version and you've got a "cowboy rib-eye."

Hands-on 1 hour, 40 minutes ★ **Total** 4 hours, including chilling time ★ **Serves 6**

GREEN CHILE SALSA VERDE

1 large poblano pepper
1 serrano pepper, seeded and chopped
½ cup chopped shallots (about 2 large)
½ cup red wine vinegar
½ cup olive oil
¼ cup chopped fresh flat-leaf parsley
¼ cup chopped fresh cilantro

2 green onions, thinly sliced
1 garlic clove, minced
1 teaspoon sugar
6 (12-ounce) rib-eye steaks
  (¾-inch-thick)
1¼ teaspoons kosher salt
1¼ teaspoons black pepper

ADOBO SAUCE

2 cups chicken broth
1 plum tomato, chopped
½ cup diced onion
2 garlic cloves, coarsely chopped
1 tablespoon sesame seeds
1 tablespoon light brown sugar
1 tablespoon raisins
1 teaspoon kosher salt
1 teaspoon ground cumin

½ teaspoon ground cinnamon
½ teaspoon black pepper
4 large dried ancho chile
  peppers, seeded
2 small dried guajillo peppers,
  stemmed and seeded
1 tablespoon apple cider vinegar
2 ounces (¼ cup) unsalted butter

1. Make the Green Chile Salsa Verde: Preheat the broiler. Line a baking sheet with aluminum foil. Broil poblano pepper on baking sheet 3 inches from heat 8 minutes or until pepper looks blistered, turning after 4 minutes. Place in a zip-top plastic freezer bag; seal and let stand 10 minutes to loosen skin. Peel; remove and discard seeds. Finely chop the pepper. Stir together poblano pepper, serrano pepper, and next 8 ingredients in a bowl. Let stand 1 hour before serving. Add salt and black pepper to taste.

2. Make the Adobo Sauce: Combine the chicken broth and next 10 ingredients in a medium saucepan over low; cook 2 minutes. Cover, remove from heat, and let stand 15 minutes. Process the broth mixture and peppers in a blender until smooth, scraping down sides as needed. Transfer the sauce to a bowl, and stir in vinegar.

3. Season the steaks with the salt and pepper; brush both sides with 1 cup of the Adobo Sauce. Cover and chill 1 to 2 hours. Remove steaks from refrigerator, and let stand at room temperature 20 minutes. Preheat the grill to 350° to 400°F (medium-high). Grill the steaks, covered with lid, 7 to 8 minutes on each side. Let stand 10 minutes before serving.

4. Meanwhile, bring remaining Adobo Sauce to a simmer in a saucepan over low; add the butter, whisking until blended. Serve with the steaks and Green Chile Salsa Verde.

GRILLED TRI-TIP WITH CITRUS-CHILE BUTTER

The tri-tip first appeared on the menu in the 1950s as a lean but tender, boneless "triangle steak." Over a relatively short amount of time, the inexpensive Santa Maria steak, as it is sometimes known, has taken the carnivorous world by storm with its lower fat content and loads of beefy flavor.

Hands-on 35 minutes ★ **Total** 40 minutes, including butter ★ **Serves** 8 to 10

2 (2-pound) tri-tip steaks*
2 teaspoons table salt
1¼ teaspoons black pepper
Citrus-Chile Butter (recipe below)

3 bunches baby Vidalia or green onions, trimmed
3 tablespoons olive oil

1. Preheat the grill to 350° to 400°F (medium-high). Sprinkle the steaks with 1½ teaspoons of the salt and 1 teaspoon of the pepper. Grill the steaks, covered with grill lid, 9 to 12 minutes on each side or to desired degree of doneness.

2. Remove from grill, and rub 3 tablespoons of the Citrus-Chile Butter onto the steaks. Cover the steaks with aluminum foil; let stand 5 minutes.

3. Meanwhile, toss the onions with the olive oil; season with remaining ½ teaspoon salt and ¼ teaspoon pepper. Grill the onions, without grill lid, 2 minutes; turn and grill 1 more minute.

4. Uncover the steaks, and cut across the grain into thin slices. Serve with the grilled onions and remaining Citrus-Chile Butter.

*Beef strip steaks (about 2 inches thick) may be substituted.

CITRUS-CHILE BUTTER

This versatile chile butter can be used as a glaze, dip, or marinade. The mellow butter is given a lively kick from the lime and jalapeño.

Hands-on 10 minutes ★ **Total** 10 minutes ★ **Makes** 1 cup

8 ounces (1 cup) butter, softened
2 tablespoons lime zest
2 tablespoons lemon zest
3 garlic cloves, minced

1 tablespoon seeded and minced jalapeño pepper
1 teaspoon chopped fresh thyme

1. Combine the first 6 ingredients. Add salt and freshly ground pepper to taste.

2. Spoon the mixture onto plastic wrap.

3. Shape into a log, and wrap with plastic wrap. Chill until ready to serve, or freeze up to 1 month.

BEEF FAJITAS

Created as a way to use up lowly scraps of meat and pay Mexican herders for working a day on the cattle ranches of South and West Texas, beef fajitas are now one of the most loved Tex-Mex dishes. The secret to this version is the marinade that gives the beef wonderful flavor and texture.

Hands-on 34 minutes ★ **Total** 3 hours, 24 minutes, including Pico de Gallo ★
Serves 6 to 8

7 tablespoons Texas Meat Rub
   (page 21)
¾ cup beer
½ cup fresh lime juice
½ cup Worcestershire sauce
⅓ cup amber agave nectar
¼ cup soy sauce

1 (3-pound) flank steak
12 to 16 (6-inch) fajita-size flour
   tortillas, warmed
Toppings: Pico de Gallo (page 35),
guacamole, shredded Cheddar
cheese, sour cream, sliced red
onions, sliced jalapeños

1. Whisk together ¼ cup of the Texas Meat Rub and next 5 ingredients in a medium saucepan. Bring to a light boil over medium; reduce heat to medium-low, and simmer, whisking constantly, 5 minutes. Remove from heat, and cool 5 minutes.

2. Place the steak in a large baking dish; pour warm marinade over the steak. Cover and chill at least 3 hours.

3. Preheat the grill to 350° to 400°F (medium-high). Remove the steak from marinade, discarding marinade. Rub both sides of the steak with remaining 3 tablespoons Texas Meat Rub.

4. Grill the steak, covered with grill lid, 3 to 5 minutes on each side or to desired degree of doneness. Remove from grill, and let stand 10 minutes. Cut the steak diagonally across the grain into thin strips. Serve the steak in warm tortillas with desired toppings.

ROSEMARY FLANK STEAK WITH FIG SALSA

Aromatic rosemary and sweet figs over savory flank steak pay delicious tribute to the Spanish padres who first brought the subtropical fruit to Texas missions.

Hands-on 30 minutes ★ **Total** 1 hour, 5 minutes ★ **Serves** 6

1 tablespoon chopped fresh
   rosemary
2 garlic cloves, minced
¾ teaspoon kosher salt
½ teaspoon freshly ground
   black pepper
3 tablespoons olive oil
1 (1¼-pound) flank steak

3 cups chopped fresh figs
1 green onion, minced
2 tablespoons chopped fresh parsley
2 tablespoons seasoned rice
   wine vinegar
3 ounces Gorgonzola cheese,
   crumbled

1. Stir together the first 4 ingredients and 1 tablespoon of the olive oil. Rub onto the steak; cover and chill 30 minutes to 4 hours.

2. Preheat the grill to 400° to 450°F (high). Toss together the figs, next 3 ingredients, and remaining 2 tablespoons oil. Add salt and pepper to taste.

3. Grill the steak, covered with grill lid, 5 minutes on each side or to desired degree of doneness. Let stand 5 minutes.

4. Cut the steak diagonally across the grain into thin strips, and arrange on a serving platter. Spoon the fig salsa over steak, and sprinkle with Gorgonzola.

TEXAS BURGERS

The secret to crafting Texas-style burgers, like any great work of art, lies in the raw materials and how they come together. Begin with ground chuck with enough fat on it to keep it juicy while cooking (about 20% fat), and mold it into rounds by hand. Using your hands helps ensure the patties do not compress too much. Add a smear of classic yellow mustard to serve them in the style of Texas-based fast-food chain Whataburger.

Hands-on 20 minutes ★ **Total** 40 minutes, including rub ★
Serves 4

1½ pounds ground chuck
2 tablespoons Worcestershire sauce
1 tablespoon Texas Meat Rub (page 21)
4 (¾-ounce) slices longhorn-style Cheddar cheese*
1 medium jalapeño pepper, thinly sliced
4 hamburger buns
2 ounces (¼ cup) butter, softened
Toppings: coarse-grained mustard, leaf lettuce, tomato slices,
    red onion slices

1. Preheat the grill to 350° to 400°F (medium-high). Shape the ground chuck into 4 (4-inch) patties. Drizzle the patties with the Worcestershire sauce, and sprinkle with Texas Meat Rub. Let stand 15 minutes.

2. Grill the patties, covered with grill lid, 2 to 3 minutes on each side or to desired degree of doneness; top with cheese. Grill, covered with grill lid, until the cheese melts. Remove from grill; top with the jalapeño, and let stand 5 minutes.

3. Butter the buns, and toast on grill. Serve the patties on toasted buns with desired toppings.

*Mild Cheddar or Colby cheese may be substituted for longhorn-style cheese.

SMOKED BARBECUE BABY BACK RIBS

Though Texas has put its mark on beef barbecue, there has always been room for pork too. For these ribs, start with a dry rub and smoke them for a while. The key is to get the meat to the point that it's really tender but not completely falling off the bone.

Hands-on 15 minutes ★ **Total** 6 hours, including rub and sauce ★ **Serves** 8

4 slabs pork baby back ribs
    (about 5 pounds)
Barbecue Rub (page 21)

3 to 4 oak, hickory, or pecan
    wood chunks
Barbecue Sauce (recipe below)

1. Rinse and pat the ribs dry. If desired, remove thin membrane from back of ribs by slicing into it with a knife and then pulling it off. (This will make ribs more tender.)

2. Coat the ribs with Barbecue Rub, and let stand 30 minutes.

3. Soak wood chunks in water 30 minutes.

4. Meanwhile, prepare smoker according to manufacturer's instructions. Place water pan in smoker; add water to depth of fill line. Bring internal temperature to 225° to 250°F for 15 to 20 minutes.

5. Drain wood chunks, and place on coals. Place the ribs, bone side up, on upper food grate; cover with smoker lid. Smoke the ribs, maintaining temperature inside smoker between 225° and 250°F, for 3 hours or until a meat thermometer inserted into thickest portion registers 180° to 185°F.

6. Remove the ribs from smoker, and baste both sides with Barbecue Sauce. Wrap ribs tightly in a double layer of heavy-duty aluminum foil, and return to smoker. Cook, bone side down, 1½ more hours.

BARBECUE SAUCE

In the Southern Belt of Texas (south through Beaumont and west toward Dallas), the meat is always served with sauce—thick, sweet, and with just a hint of heat.

1 cup thick barbecue sauce
½ cup molasses (not
    blackstrap)

2 canned chipotle peppers in
    adobo sauce, chopped

Stir together all the ingredients in a small saucepan over medium; bring to a boil, reduce heat, and simmer 10 minutes, stirring occasionally. Makes about 1½ cups

PEACH-GLAZED PORK CHOPS

Few fruits are more Southern than peaches. Turn a preserved bumper crop into a flavor-packed glaze. In the conservationist spirit of the pioneers and the native Texans before them, use up any leftover preserves to create this mouthwatering entrée.

Hands-on 31 minutes ★ **Total** 36 minutes ★ **Serves** 4

1 (18-ounce) jar peach preserves
¼ cup soy sauce
2 tablespoons grated fresh ginger
2 teaspoons olive oil
4 (8-ounce) bone-in pork loin
   chops (1½ inches thick)

¼ teaspoon table salt
¼ teaspoon freshly ground black
   pepper
4 large peaches, halved

1. Preheat grill to 350° to 400°F (medium-high). Bring the preserves, soy sauce, and ginger to a boil in a small saucepan. Remove from heat; reserve ½ cup of the preserves mixture to baste the peaches.

2. Rub the oil over pork chops; sprinkle with the salt and pepper. Grill the pork chops, covered with grill lid, 5 to 7 minutes on each side or until a meat thermometer inserted into thickest portion registers 145°F, basting often with 1 cup of the peach preserves mixture.

3. At the same time, grill the peaches, covered with grill lid, 2 to 3 minutes on each side or until tender, basting often with reserved ½ cup peach preserves mixture. Let the pork chops stand 5 minutes before serving.

PEACH PULLED PORK

This pulled pork recipe will feed a crowd, and the sweet-and-sour peach nectar celebrates the best of summer in Texas.

Hands-on 1 hour, 5 minutes ★ **Total** 10 hours ★ **Serves** 10

Peach wood chips
1 (6¼-pound) bone-in pork
   shoulder roast (Boston
   butt)
½ cup Cowgirl Pork Rub
   (page 21)

1 cup peach nectar
1 cup water
⅔ cup apple cider vinegar
1 (12-ounce) jar peach
   preserves

1. Soak the wood chips in water 30 minutes. Prepare smoker according to manufacturer's directions, bringing internal temperature to 225° to 250°F; maintain temperature for 15 to 20 minutes. Coat the roast with the Cowgirl Pork Rub, pressing gently to adhere. Let stand 30 minutes. Fill a spray bottle with peach nectar and 1 cup water.

2. Drain the wood chips, and place on coals. Place the roast on upper cooking grate; cover with smoker lid. Smoke roast, maintaining temperature inside smoker between 225° and 250°F, for 8½ hours or until a meat thermometer inserted into thickest portion registers 190° to 200°F, spraying occasionally with peach nectar mixture. Add additional water, charcoal, and wood chips as needed.

3. Remove the roast from smoker, and let stand 15 minutes. Shred or chop roast. Cook the vinegar and preserves in a small saucepan over medium-low, stirring often, until preserves are melted and mixture is smooth. Serve with the pork.

★ ★ ★

BEYOND BBQ

Hill Country Peaches

Among the many natural resources of the Texas Hill Country, the limestone-laced soils near Fredericksburg proved the perfect mix for peaches. In the early 1800s, German immigrants cultivated numerous peach orchards in the area. By the early 1900s, it was reported that there were more than 10 million peach trees in Texas, with many family orchards bearing the German heritage in their name including Vogel, Engel, Inman, Berg, and Studebaker.

PORK CHOPS WITH APRICOT-MUSTARD SAUCE

Award-winning chef Tim Byres knows a thing or two about the cowboy cuisine that became part of Texas' unique culinary identity. "It was the Wild West," Byres reminds us. "As a result, Texas food at its core is gritty. It's loud, unapologetic, high in flavor and heart, and it's all served on a plate big enough for ranch hands to devour after a hard day of working."

Hands-on 10 minutes ★ **Total** 3 hours, 50 minutes, including sauce ★
Serves 8 to 10

⅓ to ½ cup Texas Meat Rub
   (page 21)
1 (7½- to 8-pound) bone-in
   pork loin roast

Apricot-Mustard Sauce
   (recipe below)

1. Rub the Texas Meat Rub over the roast. Let stand at room temperature 1 hour.

2. Light 1 side of grill, heating to 325° to 350°F (medium); leave other side unlit. Place the pork, bone side down, over unlit side, and grill, covered, 2 to 2½ hours or until a meat thermometer inserted into thickest portion registers 145°F.

3. Remove the roast from grill, and let stand 20 minutes before cutting into individual chops. Serve with the Apricot-Mustard Sauce.

APRICOT-MUSTARD SAUCE

Hands-on 5 minutes ★ **Total** 25 minutes ★ **Makes** about 2 cups

1½ cups dried apricots
3 cups water
2 tablespoons sherry vinegar

2 tablespoons red wine vinegar
2 tablespoons Dijon mustard
1 teaspoon kosher salt

1. Bring the apricots and 3 cups water to a light boil over medium; reduce heat, and simmer 15 to 20 minutes or until the apricots are plump and soft. Stir in remaining ingredients, and cook 2 minutes. Remove from heat.

2. Process the mixture with an immersion blender until smooth. (A regular blender may be used. Let the sauce cool slightly before blending.) Add additional salt to taste.

BEER-POACHED GRILLED SAUSAGES WITH SWEET ONIONS

Central Texas' German and Czech heritage calls for Old-World-style sausage links poached in a local beer (try Shiner Bock, as used here, or Real Ale Firemans #4 Blonde Ale) and served with German mustard. While German mustards vary from region to region, you can't go wrong with Mittelscharf, a medium-hot blend of yellow and brown mustard seeds, or a sweeter, honey-infused Bavarian style. For added flavor, grill the tortillas before serving.

Hands-on 20 minutes ★ **Total** 1 hour, including rub ★ **Serves** 6

Vegetable cooking spray
6 smoked venison or pork
   sausage links*
4 (12-ounce) bottles lager beer
1 medium-size sweet onion,
   cut into ½-inch slices

1 teaspoon Texas Meat Rub
   (page 21)
6 large flour tortillas
Barbecue sauce or coarse-
   grained mustard
Garnish: grilled whole chile peppers

1. Coat cold cooking grate of grill with the cooking spray. Preheat the grill to 350° to 400°F (medium-high).

2. Bring the sausages and beer to a light boil in a Dutch oven; reduce heat to medium-low, and simmer 30 to 40 minutes or until sausages are plump.

3. Meanwhile, coat both sides of the onion slices with cooking spray, and sprinkle with the Texas Meat Rub.

4. Grill the onion slices, covered with grill lid, 8 minutes on each side or until tender and slightly charred. Transfer the onion to a bowl; cover with plastic wrap, and let steam.

5. Remove the sausages from beer. Grill the sausages, without grill lid, 12 to 14 minutes or until thoroughly cooked, turning occasionally.

6. Remove the sausages from grill, and let stand 3 to 4 minutes. Cut the onion slices in half. Serve the sausages and onions in tortillas with barbecue sauce or mustard.

*Beef sausage may be substituted.

GRILLED ANDOUILLE SAUSAGE WITH PICKLES

The Catholic French Canadian refugees who made their way from Maryland to Southeast Texas—by mistake, according to the Texas State Historical Association—settled in the "Golden Triangle" of Beaumont, Port Arthur, and Orange in 1770. They brought with them music, new holidays, a beautiful language, and, of course, delicious traditional food like andouille sausage. Made with pork and garlic, andouille became a defining staple in Cajun dining.

Hands-on 12 minutes ★ **Total** 12 minutes ★ **Serves** 4

2 pounds andouille sausage
Uncle Hoyt's Bread-and-Butter Pickles (recipe below)

Preheat the grill to 350° to 400°F (medium-high). Grill the sausage 5 minutes or until done, turning occasionally. Cut the sausage diagonally into ¼-inch-thick slices, and serve with Uncle Hoyt's Bread-and-Butter Pickles.

UNCLE HOYT'S BREAD-AND-BUTTER PICKLES

Hands-on 2 hours, 10 minutes ★ **Total** 5 hours, 20 minutes ★
Makes 14 (1-pint) jars

25 to 30 medium cucumbers
 (about 9½ pounds)
8 large onions
2 large bell peppers
½ cup pickling salt
5 cups white vinegar

4 cups sugar
2 tablespoons mustard seeds
1 teaspoon ground turmeric
½ teaspoon whole cloves
Wooden skewer

1. Cut the cucumbers into ¼-inch-thick slices and the onions into ⅛-inch-thick slices. Chop the bell peppers. Place the vegetables in a bowl; toss with pickling salt. Let stand 3 hours; drain.

2. Bring the vinegar, sugar, mustard seeds, turmeric, and cloves to a boil in a large stockpot, boiling just until sugar dissolves. Add the drained cucumber mixture, and cook, stirring often, 7 to 10 minutes or until mixture is thoroughly heated and cucumber peels turn dark green. Pack half of hot mixture in 7 (1-pint) hot, sterilized jars, filling to ½ inch from top. Remove air bubbles by gently stirring with a long wooden skewer. Cover at once with metal lids, and screw on bands. Process in boiling water bath 10 minutes. Repeat procedure with remaining mixture and 7 more hot, sterilized jars.

PECAN-CRUSTED PORK BURGERS

The pecan, Texas' official state nut harvested from Texas' official state tree, lends an irresistible crunch to this delicious burger. If you can't find ground pork in your local supermarket, ask your butcher to grind it for you.

Hands-on 27 minutes ★ **Total** 52 minutes, including mayonnaise ★ **Serves 4**

Vegetable cooking spray
1½ pounds lean ground pork
2 tablespoons reserved
    mayonnaise mixture
    from Dried Apricot-Chipotle
    Mayonnaise
1 tablespoon butter, melted

½ cup finely chopped pecans
½ teaspoon table salt
¼ teaspoon black pepper
4 French hamburger buns, split
4 Bibb lettuce leaves
Dried Apricot-Chipotle Mayonnaise
    (recipe below)

1. Coat cold cooking grate of grill with the cooking spray, and place on grill. Preheat grill to 350° to 400°F (medium-high).

2. Gently combine the pork and reserved 2 tablespoons mayonnaise mixture until blended, using hands. Shape into 4 (4-inch-wide, 1-inch-thick) patties.

3. Whisk together the butter and next 3 ingredients in a small bowl until well blended. Sprinkle each patty with about 2 tablespoons pecan mixture (about 1 tablespoon on each side), pressing gently to adhere.

4. Grill the pecan-covered pork patties, covered with grill lid, 6 to 8 minutes on each side or until a meat thermometer inserted into centers registers 145°F. Grill the buns, cut sides down, 1 to 2 minutes or until lightly toasted. Serve the burgers on buns with lettuce and Dried Apricot-Chipotle Mayonnaise.

DRIED APRICOT-CHIPOTLE MAYONNAISE

Tart lime juice and smoky chipotle help to balance the fruit's intense sweetness.

Hands-on 10 minutes ★ **Total** 25 minutes ★ **Makes** about 1 cup

½ cup dried apricots
¼ cup hot water
2 tablespoons fresh lime juice
½ cup mayonnaise
1 canned chipotle chile pepper
    in adobo sauce, chopped

2 tablespoons finely chopped green
    onion
1 tablespoon adobo sauce from can

1. Combine the dried apricots, hot water, and lime juice in a bowl. Let stand 15 minutes; drain. Pat apricots dry, and coarsely chop.

2. Combine the mayonnaise and next 3 ingredients; reserve 2 tablespoons of the mixture for the Pecan-Crusted Pork Burgers. Stir the apricots into remaining mayonnaise mixture. Cover and chill until ready to serve. Makes about 1 cup

SMOKED CHICKEN

Piloncillo is a raw sugar made from reduced cane juice. It's sold molded into cone shapes and is sometimes labeled panela. To measure, place the cone in a zip-top plastic freezer bag, and pound it with a meat mallet to break it apart.

Hands-on 15 minutes ★ **Total** 4 hours, 5 minutes ★ **Serves** 12

3 to 4 oak, hickory, or pecan wood chunks
1 cup firmly packed piloncillo (Mexican brown
    sugar) (about 1 [8-ounce] cone)*
1 tablespoon ancho chile powder
1 tablespoon table salt
1 tablespoon freshly ground black pepper
4 (3¾- to 4-pound) whole chickens

1. Soak the wood chunks in water to cover 1 hour.

2. Meanwhile, combine the piloncillo and next 3 ingredients in a small bowl. Rub the chickens with the piloncillo mixture, and let stand 30 minutes.

3. Prepare the smoker according to manufacturer's directions. Place water pan in smoker; add water to depth of fill line. Bring internal temperature to 225° to 250°F, and maintain temperature 15 to 20 minutes.

4. Drain the wood chunks, and place on coals. Place the chickens on cooking grate; cover with smoker lid. Smoke 2½ to 3 hours or until a meat thermometer inserted into thickest portion of thighs registers 165°F.

5. Remove the chickens from smoker, and let stand 20 minutes before slicing.

Dark brown sugar may be substituted for piloncillo.

Pollos Asados Los Norteños
San Antonio
◇◇◇◇◇◇◇◇

For traditional Mexican-style charcoal-grilled chicken, this is one of San Antonio's hidden gems. With a simple dining room of red-checkered tablecloths, a self-serve condiment station, and plastic baskets of food, there's nothing formal about this place. But that doesn't keep people from driving across the city to enjoy the great food.

The key to delicious chicken is keeping it tender and juicy, something this favored little hole-in-the-wall has mastered with seemingly effortless skill. An order of a whole chicken comes with rice, tortillas, half of a grilled onion, and grilled jalapeño.

*4642 Rigsby Ave
San Antonio, TX 78222
210-648-3303*

DRY-BRINED BEER-CAN CHICKEN

Beer-can chicken is truly a testament to human ingenuity. Drink half a can of beer (okay, maybe two-and-a-half cans) and use the remaining half can to vertically cook a whole chicken to a crispy, crackly, evenly browned perfection.

Hands-on 30 minutes ★ **Total** 2 hours, 10 minutes, plus 1 day chilling time ★
Serves 8

¼ cup kosher salt
1 tablespoon light brown sugar
2 teaspoons pimentón (sweet smoked Spanish paprika)
1½ teaspoons dried marjoram or oregano
1 teaspoon dried thyme

1 teaspoon freshly ground black pepper
3 bay leaves, finely crumbled
2 (3½- to 4-pound) whole chickens
1 large oven bag
2 (12-ounce) cans brown ale

1. Combine the first 7 ingredients in a small bowl. Sprinkle skin and cavities of the chickens with salt mixture. Place the chickens in oven bag; twist end of bag, and close with tie. Chill 24 hours.

2. Light 1 side of grill, heating to 350° to 400°F (medium-high); leave other side unlit. Reserve ½ cup beer from each can for another use. Place each chicken upright onto a beer can, fitting into cavity. Pull legs forward to form a tripod, allowing chickens to stand upright.

3. Place the chickens upright on unlit side of grill. Grill, covered with grill lid, 1 hour and 30 minutes to 1 hour and 40 minutes or until golden and a meat thermometer inserted into thickest portion registers 165°F. Let stand 10 minutes. Carefully remove chickens from cans; cut into quarters.

MARINATED CHICKEN QUARTERS

Delicious white meat marinated in lemon juice, garlic, and a savory blend of spices is an easy, yet impressive, beginning to your next family feast.

Hands-on 1 hour ★ **Total** 1 hour, plus 8 hours chilling time ★ **Serves** 4

4 ounces (½ cup) butter, melted
½ cup fresh lemon juice
1 tablespoon paprika
1 tablespoon dried oregano
1 teaspoon garlic salt
1 tablespoon chopped fresh cilantro

1 teaspoon ground cumin
1 (2½-pound) whole chicken, quartered
½ teaspoon table salt
½ teaspoon ground black pepper

1. Whisk together the first 7 ingredients; reserve ½ cup of the butter mixture for basting, and chill.

2. Sprinkle the chicken with the salt and pepper. Place in a shallow dish or zip-top plastic freezer bag; pour remaining butter mixture over chicken. Cover or seal, and chill 8 hours.

3. Preheat the grill to 350° to 400°F (medium-high). Remove the chicken from marinade; discard marinade. Grill, covered with grill lid, 40 to 45 minutes or until done, basting often with reserved butter mixture and turning once.

SMOKED CHICKEN TORTILLA SOUP

If variety is indeed the spice of life, a truly versatile Texan chef will not shy away from experimenting with the wide bounty of cultivars from the chile pepper family, including New Mexican breeds. The New Mexico chile powder in this recipe and the smoked chicken add a rich flavor dynamic to this well-known soup.

Hands-on 25 minutes ★ **Total** 1 hour, 20 minutes ★ **Serves** 8 to 10

1 large onion, diced
1 large jalapeño pepper, seeded
    and chopped
3 tablespoons olive oil
3 garlic cloves, chopped
8 cups chicken broth
1 (15.25-ounce) can whole
    kernel corn, drained*
1 (15-ounce) can black beans,
    drained
1 (14.5-ounce) can fire-roasted
    diced tomatoes
1 (14.5-ounce) can diced
    tomatoes with chiles

3 tablespoons ground cumin
1½ tablespoons New Mexico
    chile powder
1½ teaspoons table salt
1 teaspoon Worcestershire sauce
5 cups coarsely chopped
    Smoked Chicken (page 99)
Toppings: tortilla strips, fresh
    cilantro, avocado slices, lime
    slices, crumbled queso
    fresco (fresh Mexican
    cheese)

1. Sauté the onion and jalapeño pepper in hot oil in a Dutch oven over medium-high 5 to 6 minutes. Add the garlic, and sauté 1 to 2 minutes.

2. Stir in the broth and next 8 ingredients. Bring to a boil; reduce heat, and simmer 40 minutes.

3. Remove from heat, and stir in the chicken. Let stand 10 minutes before serving. Serve with desired toppings.

*3 to 4 ears fresh corn may be substituted for canned corn. Remove the husks, and cut kernels from cobs.

CHICKEN-BRISKET BRUNSWICK STEW

Looking for a way to make the most of leftover brisket? Transform it into an aromatic, bone-sticking game-day stew that is an instant crowd-pleaser. Add a splash of hot sauce to really give it some Texan heat.

Hands-on 30 minutes ★ **Total** 2 hours, 40 minutes ★ **Makes** 16 cups

2 large onions, chopped
2 garlic cloves, minced
1 tablespoon vegetable oil
1½ tablespoons jarred beef
    soup base
2 cups water
2 pounds skinned and boned
    chicken breasts
1 (28-ounce) can fire-roasted
    crushed tomatoes
1 (12-ounce) package frozen
    white shoepeg or whole
    kernel corn
1 (10-ounce) package frozen
    cream-style corn, thawed

1 (9-ounce) package frozen
    baby lima beans
1 (12-ounce) bottle chili sauce
1 tablespoon brown sugar
1 tablespoon yellow mustard
1 tablespoon Worcestershire sauce
½ teaspoon coarsely ground
    black pepper
1 pound chopped Texas Smoked
    Brisket (page 61)
1 tablespoon fresh lemon juice
Hot sauce (optional)

1. Sauté the onion and garlic in hot oil in a 7½-quart Dutch oven over medium-high 3 to 5 minutes or until tender. Combine the soup base and 2 cups water; add to Dutch oven. Add the chicken and next 9 ingredients. Bring to a boil. Cover, reduce heat to low, and cook, stirring occasionally, 2 hours.

2. Uncover and shred chicken into large pieces using 2 forks. Stir in the brisket and lemon juice. Cover and cook 10 minutes. Serve with the hot sauce, if desired.

ANDOUILLE SAUSAGE AND SMOKED CHICKEN GUMBO

Another dish Texas can thank Cajun Louisiana for, gumbo gets its name from the West African word quingombo, *which means okra. Today, gumbo takes many forms, shape-shifting to satisfy the tastes of an ever-changing culinary landscape.*

Hands-on 1 hour ★ **Total** 1 hour, 40 minutes, not including Smoked Chicken ★ **Serves** 6

11 ounces (⅔ cup) butter
½ pound andouille sausage, halved lengthwise and cut into ¼-inch-thick slices
¾ cup (3.19 ounces) all-purpose flour
1 green bell pepper, finely chopped
1 large onion, finely chopped
3 celery ribs, finely chopped
4 garlic cloves, minced
1 teaspoon table salt
1 teaspoon freshly ground black pepper
4 cups chicken broth
1 (14½-ounce) can diced tomatoes
1 teaspoon dried oregano
1 teaspoon dried thyme
2 bay leaves
2½ cups shredded Smoked Chicken (page 99)
Garnish: sliced green onions

1. Melt 1 tablespoon of the butter in a Dutch oven over medium. Cook the sausage in butter 6 minutes or until browned; remove sausage with a slotted spoon, and drain on paper towels, reserving drippings in Dutch oven. Add remaining butter to Dutch oven. Gradually whisk in the flour; cook, whisking constantly, until flour is a milk chocolate color (about 25 minutes).

2. Stir in the bell pepper and next 5 ingredients; cook, stirring constantly, 15 minutes or until vegetables are tender. Gradually add the broth, stirring until combined. Add the tomatoes, oregano, thyme, and bay leaves. Bring to a light boil; reduce heat to low, and simmer, stirring occasionally, 30 minutes or until slightly thickened.

3. Return the sausage to pan; simmer, stirring occasionally, 15 minutes. Stir in the Smoked Chicken. Remove and discard bay leaves before serving.

Note: Substitute smoked chicken from your favorite barbecue restaurant, or use shredded deli rotisserie chicken for the Smoked Chicken.

★ ★ ★
BEYOND BBQ

Cajun Culture

Along the coast, Jefferson County, which lies on the state's eastern border with Louisiana, is rooted in Cajun culture. A second wave of Western Louisianans crossed into Texas in the 1950s to move closer to oil refinery centers in Beaumont, Port Arthur, and Orange. They brought the traditional dishes and cooking methods that have made a flavorful mark on the Lone Star State.

SMOKY CHICKEN BBQ KABOBS

A tradition usually credited to Alabama is gaining popularity in Texas and beyond. It's white barbecue sauce, and it's coming for your taste buds. Tangy, zesty, and creamy, white barbecue sauce complements the smoke on the tender chicken.

Hands-on 25 minutes ★ **Total** 25 minutes, including sauce ★ **Serves** 8

4 skinned and boned chicken
    breasts (about 2 pounds)
½ large red onion, cut into fourths
    and separated into pieces

1 pint cherry tomatoes
8 (8-inch) metal skewers
Smoky-Sweet BBQ Rub (page 20)
White BBQ Sauce (recipe below)

1. Preheat the grill to 350° to 400°F (medium-high). Cut the chicken into 1-inch cubes. Thread the chicken, onion, and tomatoes alternately onto skewers, leaving ¼ inch between pieces. Sprinkle the kabobs with the Smoky-Sweet BBQ Rub.

2. Grill the kabobs, covered with grill lid, 4 to 5 minutes on each side. Serve with the White BBQ Sauce.

WHITE BBQ SAUCE

Hands-on 5 minutes ★ **Total** 5 minutes ★ **Makes** 1¾ cups

1½ cups mayonnaise
⅓ cup white vinegar
1 teaspoon freshly ground
    black pepper

½ teaspoon table salt
½ teaspoon sugar
1 garlic clove, pressed

Stir together all the ingredients in a small bowl. Store in the refrigerator.

CHICKEN FAJITAS

Fajitas are a dominant Tex-Mex meal in West Texas with roots in the Rio Grande Valley. The Houston Chronicle *speculated that an increase in demand for the sizzling, build-it-yourself meal and a bend toward healthier dining options led to restaurants swapping out skirt steak for grilled chicken strips.*

Hands-on 30 minutes ★ **Total** 2 hours, 30 minutes, including guacamole ★ **Serves** 6 to 8

½ cup white wine Worcestershire sauce
½ cup dry white wine
½ cup soy sauce
5 skinned and boned chicken breasts
¼ cup Texas Meat Rub (page 21)

12 to 16 (6-inch) fajita-size flour or corn tortillas, warmed
Toppings: Pico de Gallo (page 35), Simple Guacamole (recipe below), shredded Cheddar cheese, sour cream

1. Stir together the first 3 ingredients. Pour the marinade into a large shallow dish or zip-top plastic freezer bag; add the chicken. Cover or seal, and chill 2 hours, turning once.

2. Preheat the grill to 350° to 400°F (medium-high). Remove the chicken from marinade, discarding marinade. Rub the chicken with the Texas Meat Rub. Grill the chicken, covered with grill lid, 5 to 6 minutes on each side or until done. Remove the chicken from grill, and let stand 10 minutes. Cut the chicken diagonally across the grain into thin strips. Serve the chicken in warm tortillas with desired toppings.

SIMPLE GUACAMOLE

Hands-on 5 minutes ★ **Total** 5 minutes ★ **Makes** 3 cups

5 medium-size ripe avocados, halved
2 tablespoons fresh lime juice

½ cup diced red onion
¾ teaspoon kosher salt
1 garlic clove, pressed

Scoop the avocado pulp into a large bowl; mash with a fork just until chunky. Stir in the lime juice and remaining ingredients.

★ ★ ★ BEYOND BBQ

Corn Tortillas

When it comes to ingredients most easily cultivated in Mexico, and by extension in South Texas, corn is a key commodity. The most common use for corn is in the form of tortillas. Spanish for "little cakes," tortillas were originally made from corn that was cooked with water and lime to remove the husks and then ground on a metate, a three-legged stone table. What was left was a dense dough called masa. The masa was rolled into a ball, pressed into a flat round using a tortilla press, and either heated on a flat cast-iron comal or griddle, or fried until crispy.

KING RANCH CHICKEN

You can't attend a church supper, potluck, wedding shower, or swap meet in South Texas without encountering this gooey, cheesy, spicy casserole dish.

Hands-on 1 hour ★ **Total** 1 hour, 40 minutes ★ **Serves** 12

Vegetable cooking spray
3 ounces (6 tablespoons) butter
1½ cups chopped onion
1 cup chopped red bell pepper
1 cup chopped poblano peppers
  (about 2 medium peppers)
1 jalapeño pepper, seeded and
  chopped
2 garlic cloves, chopped
1 tablespoon chili powder
1 tablespoon ground cumin
1 teaspoon kosher salt
½ teaspoon freshly ground
  black pepper
¼ cup (1.06 ounces) all-purpose flour
1¾ cups chicken broth

1 (10-ounce) can diced tomatoes with
  green chiles, drained
1½ cups sour cream
2 pounds Smoked Chicken
  (page 99), coarsely chopped
  (about 5 cups)
1 cup loosely packed fresh
  cilantro leaves, chopped
2 cups shredded Monterey Jack
  cheese
2 cups shredded sharp Cheddar
  cheese
18 (6-inch) corn tortillas
¼ cup canola oil
Garnish: chopped fresh cilantro

1. Preheat the oven to 375°F. Lightly grease a 13- x 9-inch baking dish with cooking spray. Melt the butter in a large skillet over medium-high. Add the onion and next 3 ingredients; sauté 8 to 10 minutes or until tender and lightly browned. Add the garlic, chili powder, cumin, salt, and pepper, and cook 1 minute.

2. Sprinkle the flour over the vegetable mixture, and cook, stirring constantly, 1 minute. Whisk in the broth, and bring to a boil, stirring constantly. Boil 1 to 2 minutes or until thickened. Remove from heat. Add the tomatoes and sour cream. Stir together the chicken and cilantro; stir in the vegetable mixture until blended. Combine the cheeses in a small bowl.

3. Heat a large cast-iron skillet over high. Lightly brush each tortilla on both sides with oil. Cook the tortillas, in batches, in hot skillet until lightly browned and crisp on both sides.

4. Line the bottom of prepared baking dish with 6 tortillas, overlapping slightly, to cover bottom of dish. Top with half of the chicken mixture and one-third of the cheese. Repeat layers once. Top with remaining tortillas and cheese. Lightly coat a sheet of aluminum foil with cooking spray, and cover baking dish.

5. Bake at 375°F for 20 minutes. Uncover and bake 10 more minutes or until bubbly and lightly browned on top. Let stand 10 minutes before serving.

BBQ OYSTERS WITH TWO BUTTERS

Jack Gilmore's method of grilling Texas Gulf oysters with a duo of flavored butters is pretty spectacular. Smoke from the grill adds a nice dimension to the oysters' brininess. Caution when handling these: Don't douse yourself with the hot melted butter.

Hands-on 20 minutes ★ **Total** 4 hours, 45 minutes, including butters ★
Serves 10 to 12

BACON AND CAYENNE BUTTER

2 bacon slices, cut into ½-inch pieces
4 ounces (½ cup) unsalted butter, softened
1 tablespoon chopped fresh flat-leaf parsley
1 tablespoon chopped fresh cilantro
1 tablespoon chopped garlic
2 tablespoons pale ale beer, such as Peacemaker Extra Pale Ale

1 tablespoon fresh lemon juice
½ teaspoon kosher salt
½ teaspoon freshly ground black pepper
¼ teaspoon ground red pepper
Dash of Worcestershire sauce

CHIPOTLE BUTTER

2 tablespoons bourbon
1 teaspoon brown sugar
4 ounces (½ cup) unsalted butter, softened

1 tablespoon fresh lime juice
1 tablespoon chopped garlic
2 canned chipotle peppers in adobo sauce

2 dozen large fresh oysters on the half shell

1. Make the Bacon and Cayenne Butter: Cook the bacon in a medium skillet over medium, stirring often, 6 to 8 minutes or until crisp; remove bacon, and drain on paper towels, discarding drippings in skillet. Cool 5 minutes.

2. Process the bacon, butter, and next 9 ingredients in a food processor until smooth, stopping to scrape down sides as needed. Cover and chill 4 to 6 hours.

3. Make the Chipotle Butter: Combine the bourbon and brown sugar in a medium bowl, stirring until sugar dissolves.

4. Process the bourbon mixture, butter, and next 3 ingredients in a food processor until smooth, stopping to scrape down sides as needed. Cover and chill 4 to 6 hours. (Butters may be shaped into logs with plastic wrap and frozen up to 1 month.)

5. Preheat grill to 450°F (high). Arrange the oysters in a single layer on grill. Spoon 2 teaspoons Bacon and Cayenne Butter or Chipotle Butter into each oyster; grill, without grill lid, 7 minutes or until edges curl. Serve immediately.

CARIBBEAN SHRIMP KABOBS

The Texas Gulf is teeming with schools of pink, brown, and white shrimp. From Beaumont to Brownsville, catching shrimp is both a livelihood and a way of life. Marinated, skewered, and grilled, these diminutive crustaceans are a juicy, succulent, no-fuss main dish.

Hands-on 19 minutes ★ **Total** 49 minutes ★ **Serves** 4

1 cup fresh orange juice
¼ cup fresh lime juice
¼ cup chopped fresh cilantro
¼ cup olive oil
½ teaspoon table salt
½ teaspoon chili powder
4 garlic cloves, minced
1½ pounds peeled and deveined large
    raw shrimp with tails
4 (12-inch) metal or wooden skewers
Garnishes: orange slices, lime wedges

1. Whisk together the first 7 ingredients in a large shallow dish or zip-top plastic freezer bag; add shrimp. Cover or seal, and chill 30 minutes. Preheat grill to 350° to 400°F (medium-high). Remove the shrimp from marinade, reserving marinade. Thread the shrimp onto skewers.

2. Grill the shrimp, covered with grill lid, 2 minutes on each side or just until shrimp turn pink. Meanwhile, bring reserved marinade to a boil in a small saucepan, and cook 5 minutes. Remove from heat; drizzle over grilled shrimp.

Note: If using wooden skewers, soak them in water for 30 minutes before assembling the kabobs.

★ ★ ★
LONE STAR LEGENDS

King's Inn
Baffin Bay
◇◇◇◇◇◇◇◇◇

Topping the list for Gulf Coast anglers, Baffin Bay is a popular seaside destination and home to one of the state's classic seafood restaurants, the King's Inn in the town of Riviera. Since 1945, the King's Inn has served up a wide range of fresh-catch dishes from fried shrimp to pan-sautéed snapper. Don't let the white tablecloths fool you; this is a friendly casual spot. Its local fame draws quite a crowd on weekends and holidays, though, so you may want to make a reservation.

1116 S. County Rd 2270
Riviera, TX 78379
361-297-5265
baffinbaytx.com

TEXAS GULF FISH TACOS

The Texas shoreline is one of the country's most valuable resources. Shrimp, oysters, and native redfish thrive among the wetlands and inlet bays, while the Gulf of Mexico's ocean basin provides ample room for anglers to find mahi-mahi, amberjack, and yellowfin tuna.

Hands-on 25 minutes ★ **Total** 50 minutes, including slaw and mayo ★
Serves 4 to 6

2 tablespoons white wine vinegar
2 teaspoons canola oil
½ teaspoon table salt
¼ teaspoon freshly ground
   black pepper
4 cups shredded cabbage
½ cup chopped fresh cilantro
4 green onions, chopped
Vegetable cooking spray
4 (6-ounce) skinless mahi-mahi
   fillets

2 teaspoons canola oil
2 teaspoons ancho chile powder
½ teaspoon table salt
½ teaspoon freshly ground
   black pepper
¼ teaspoon dried Mexican oregano
¼ teaspoon ground cumin
12 corn tortillas
Spicy Chipotle Mayo (recipe below)
Lime wedges
Garnish: fresh cilantro

1. Whisk together vinegar and next 3 ingredients in a large bowl. Add cabbage, cilantro, and green onions; toss to coat. Cover and chill until ready to assemble tacos.

2. Coat cold cooking grate with cooking spray, and place on grill. Preheat the grill to 350° to 400°F (medium-high). Rub both sides of the fish with oil.

3. Stir together the ancho chile powder and next 4 ingredients; rub chile powder mixture evenly over both sides of fish, pressing gently to adhere.

4. Grill the fish, covered with grill lid, 4 to 5 minutes on each side. Remove and cover with foil; keep warm.

5. Grill the tortillas, in batches, 10 to 20 seconds on each side, and wrap in aluminum foil.

6. Flake the fish into bite-size pieces, and serve in grilled tortillas with the slaw, Spicy Chipotle Mayo, and lime wedges.

SPICY CHIPOTLE MAYO

Hands-on 5 minutes ★ **Total** 5 minutes ★ **Makes** ¾ cup

¾ cup mayonnaise
1 tablespoon minced canned chipotle
   pepper in adobo sauce

1 tablespoon fresh lime juice
1 garlic clove, minced

Stir together all the ingredients. Cover and chill until ready to serve. Refrigerate in an airtight container up to 1 week.

CRAB-STUFFED CATFISH FILLETS

This delectable main dish celebrates two Southern favorites—catfish and crab—elevating them with a tasty rémoulade loaded with Cajun flavor.

Hands-on 40 minutes ★ **Total** 1 hour, 35 minutes ★ **Serves** 6

½ cup butter
3 celery ribs, diced
1 small onion, diced
1 small green bell pepper, diced
1 tablespoon minced garlic
1 tablespoon fresh lemon juice
2 teaspoons Cajun seasoning
⅛ teaspoon hot sauce
1 cup panko (Japanese breadcrumbs)

½ pound fresh lump crabmeat, drained
6 (7-oz.) fresh catfish fillets
1 tablespoon olive oil
1 teaspoon paprika
Table salt
Freshly ground black pepper
Cajun Rémoulade (recipe below)

1. Melt butter in a large skillet over medium-high; add celery and next 3 ingredients, and sauté 6 minutes or until tender. Stir in lemon juice and next 2 ingredients, and cook 1 minute. Gently stir in breadcrumbs, crabmeat, and, if desired, additional Cajun seasoning and hot sauce. Remove from heat; cool completely (about 15 minutes).

2. Preheat oven to 425°F. Butterfly catfish fillets by making a lengthwise cut in 1 side, carefully cutting to but not through the opposite side; unfold fillets. Spoon crab mixture down center of 1 side of each butterflied fillet; fold opposite side over filling. Brush fillets with olive oil; sprinkle with paprika and desired amount of salt and pepper. Place fillets on a wire rack coated with cooking spray in a jelly-roll pan.

3. Bake at 425°F for 20 to 25 minutes or until fish flakes with a fork. Serve with Cajun Rémoulade.

BARBECUE RÉMOULADE

Hands-on 5 minutes ★ **Total** 5 minutes ★ **Makes** 2 cups

½ cup dill pickle relish, drained
½ cup mayonnaise
¼ cup diced yellow onion
¼ cup diced celery
¼ cup diced red bell pepper
¼ cup chopped fresh flat-leaf parsley
3 tablespoons Texas Barbecue Sauce (page 24)

3 tablespoons yellow mustard
2 tablespoons minced garlic
2 tablespoons Creole mustard
2 tablespoons prepared horseradish
2 tablespoons fresh lemon juice
3 dashes hot sauce
Table salt
Freshly ground black pepper

Process first 13 ingredients and salt and pepper to taste in a food processor 30 to 40 seconds or until finely chopped. Serve immediately or chilled.

GRILLED REDFISH WITH CILANTRO-SERRANO CHIMICHURRI

Sartin's Seafood Restaurant

Nederland

◇◇◇◇◇◇◇◇◇

For a truly Coastal Texas experience, there's no better place to try Texas barbecued crab than at Sartin's. The tasty little crustaceans alone are why people drive from hours away to visit. The atmosphere is friendly and down-home. Enjoy a big order of barbecue crabs, or get a whole plate of crabs—both barbecued and stuffed—along with catfish and batter-fried Gulf shrimp.

3520 Nederland Ave
Nederland, TX 77627
409-721-9420
sartins.com

Fishing for redfish in the flats along the Gulf Coast is a spiritual experience for most Texas anglers. There's something about taking a trip down to the bay and bringing home a cooler of fresh fish to cook on the grill. Any mild flaky fish works well in this recipe, and the chimichurri is the perfect sauce to bring out the natural flavor.

Hands-on 20 minutes ★ **Total** 30 minutes, not including rice ★
Serves 4

1 (1¼-pound) skinless redfish fillet
Vegetable cooking spray
1 teaspoon table salt
1 teaspoon freshly ground black pepper
Juice of ½ lemon
1 cup chopped fresh cilantro
½ cup extra virgin olive oil
2 serrano peppers, seeded and coarsely chopped
5 green onions, coarsely chopped
3 garlic cloves, coarsely chopped
2 tablespoons fresh lime juice
Green Rice (page 150)
Garnish: fresh cilantro

1. Preheat the grill to 400° to 450°F (high). Coat the fish lightly with cooking spray; sprinkle with ½ teaspoon of the salt, ½ teaspoon of the pepper, and lemon juice.

2. Process the cilantro, remaining salt and pepper, olive oil, and next 4 ingredients in a food processor until slightly chunky.

3. Place the fish on grill rack coated with cooking spray. Grill the fish, covered with grill lid, 6 minutes on each side or until fish flakes with a fork. Serve over the Green Rice with the sauce.

SPECTACULAR SIDES

TOMATO, AVOCADO, AND COTIJA SALAD

The "Parmesan of Mexico," Cotija cheese is a crumbly cousin to Parmigiano-Reggiano and often compared in flavor to salty feta. Named for the town in the Mexican state of Michoacán, the strong, briny taste of Cotija makes it great for sprinkling over grilled vegetables, salads, tacos, and soups.

Hands-on 20 minutes ★ **Total** 45 minutes ★ **Serves** 4 to 6

5 plum tomatoes, quartered
½ teaspoon table salt
2 ripe avocados, cubed
½ cup chopped fresh cilantro
1 jalapeño pepper, seeded and
    finely chopped
1 garlic clove, pressed

2 tablespoons extra virgin
    olive oil
1 tablespoon fresh lime juice
½ teaspoon freshly ground
    black pepper
½ cup crumbled Cotija cheese*

1. Toss together the tomatoes and salt; drain on a paper towel-lined baking sheet 15 minutes.

2. Combine the tomatoes, avocados, and next 6 ingredients in a large bowl. Let stand 10 to 15 minutes. Sprinkle with the cheese, and serve immediately.

*Feta cheese may be substituted for Cotija cheese.

GRAPEFRUIT, AVOCADO, AND BUTTER LETTUCE SALAD

In the winter, the Rio Grande Valley is alive with orchards of juicy red grapefruit. Tender butter lettuce paired with creamy avocado slices, toasted pine nuts, and the brightness of grapefruit is a fantastic combination everyone is sure to love.

Hands-on 20 minutes ★ **Total** 20 minutes ★ **Serves** 6 to 8

2 large red grapefruit
2 heads butter lettuce, torn
2 ripe avocados, sliced

⅓ cup toasted pine nuts
Citrus Vinaigrette (recipe below)
Garnish: fresh cilantro leaves

1. Using a sharp, thin-bladed knife, cut a ¼-inch-thick slice from each end of each grapefruit. Place flat-end down on a cutting board, and remove peel in strips, cutting from top to bottom following the curvature of fruit. Remove any bitter white pith. Holding peeled grapefruit in the palm of your hand, slice between membranes, and gently remove whole segments.

2. Divide lettuce among 6 to 8 serving plates. Top each serving with grapefruit segments and avocado slices; sprinkle with pine nuts. Drizzle with desired amount of Citrus Vinaigrette, and add salt and pepper to taste.

CITRUS VINAIGRETTE

Hands-on 5 minutes ★ **Total** 5 minutes ★ **Makes** ⅔ cup

¼ cup fresh orange juice
2 Tbsp. fresh lime juice
½ tsp. sugar

½ tsp. table salt
¼ tsp. freshly ground black pepper
¼ cup olive oil

Whisk together the first 5 ingredients in a small bowl. Add oil in a slow, steady stream, whisking until smooth. Refrigerate in an airtight container up to 5 days.

Koolsla, Cold Slaugh, or Coleslaw?

Coleslaw has been around as long as people have been writing cookbooks. In fact, the ancient Romans of the 5th century AD recorded a recipe of shredded cabbage, vinegar, and eggs in the ancient cookbook attributed to Apicius. It wasn't until the Dutch settled New Amsterdam in the 17th century that coleslaw reached the shores of North America in the form of *koolsla*—in Dutch, *kool* means "cabbage" and *sla* means "salad." By the 1800s, when the recipe began showing up in American cookbooks, the name was twisted into "cold slaw," sometimes spelled "cold slaugh." From that malaprop was born an alternative dish recorded in 1839's *The Kentucky Housewife* that would make coleslaw purists reel: Hot Slaugh!

CHIPOTLE-CILANTRO SLAW

Barbecue with a side of slaw is one of those divine pairings—like fried chicken with potato salad or hamburgers with French fries—that mere mortals have the privilege of enjoying in wide-eyed wonder. This coleslaw gets a Texas-sized flavor boost from piquant chile peppers and cilantro.

Hands-on 15 minutes ★ **Total** 15 minutes ★ **Serves** 6 to 8

¼ cup mayonnaise
1 tablespoon sugar
2 tablespoons sour cream
1 teaspoon lime zest
2 tablespoons fresh lime juice
2 teaspoons red wine vinegar
½ teaspoon table salt
½ teaspoon ground black pepper

1 (16-ounce) package shredded coleslaw mix
1 carrot, shredded
2 canned chipotle chile peppers in adobo sauce, finely chopped
½ cup minced fresh cilantro

Whisk together the first 8 ingredients in a large bowl. Add the coleslaw mix and remaining ingredients, and stir until coated. Serve immediately, or cover and chill up to 1 hour.

LONE STAR SLAW

Sectioned grapefruit, toasted pecans, and herbs are stirred into this refreshing slaw, giving it an extra dose of Texas flavor.

Hands-on 15 minutes ★ **Total** 15 minutes ★ **Serves** 6

¼ cup apple cider vinegar
¼ cup canola oil
2 tablespoons mayonnaise
1 tablespoon honey
½ teaspoon salt
¼ teaspoon pepper
¼ teaspoon celery seeds
1 (16-ounce) package shredded coleslaw mix

½ teaspoon grapefruit zest
2 tablespoons fresh grapefruit juice
1 grapefruit, sectioned
¾ cup toasted chopped pecans
1 tablespoon chopped fresh cilantro

Whisk together vinegar, canola oil, mayonnaise, honey, salt, pepper, and celery seeds in a large bowl. Stir in coleslaw mix, grapefruit zest, grapefruit juice, grapefruit sections, toasted pecans, and chopped fresh cilantro. Serve immediately, or chill and serve.

CHIPOTLE GRILLED CORN

The advanced Mesoamerican civilizations of pre-Columbian Mexico knew the value of corn, or maize. In fact, the Mayan myth describes how all of mankind was created from corn kernels. The Europeans who explored Mexico and North America were quick to capitalize on this golden grain. Enjoy this satisfying side dish off the cob, too, as a base for the Black Bean and Grilled Corn Salad (page 138).

Hands-on 36 minutes ★ **Total** 36 minutes ★ **Serves** 8

4 ounces (½ cup) unsalted butter, melted
2 tablespoons chipotle hot sauce
1 tablespoon fresh lime juice
Vegetable cooking spray

8 ears fresh corn, husks removed
½ teaspoon kosher salt
¼ teaspoon coarsely ground black pepper

1. Preheat the grill to 350° to 400°F (medium-high). Stir together the butter, hot sauce, and lime juice in a bowl.

2. Lightly coat the corn with cooking spray. Grill the corn, covered with grill lid, 15 to 20 minutes or until tender, turning every 5 minutes. Brush the corn evenly with butter mixture; sprinkle with salt and pepper.

★ ★ ★

BEYOND BBQ

The Black Beans of Huerta

While black beans have been an integral source of nutrition for Americans since the earliest natives walked the continent, in the history of Texas, the legume played a much more ominous role. After the founding of the Republic of Texas, the country was still having its share of problems with Mexican president Santa Anna and his troops. In 1843, when 176 Texan soldiers escaped and were recaptured by Col. Domingo Huerta, it was decided that every 10th prisoner would be executed. The prisoners were forced, one by one, to draw beans from an earthen jar. Those who drew a white bean would live, but those who drew a black bean were sentenced to death.

BLACK BEAN AND GRILLED CORN SALAD

Black beans tossed with sweet grilled corn create a rib-sticking side dish that can accompany tacos, burgers, or fish.

Hands-on: 8 minutes ★ Total: 8 minutes ★ Serves 6

¼ cup apple cider vinegar
3 tablespoons chopped fresh
    cilantro
2 tablespoons canola oil
½ teaspoon table salt
½ teaspoon sugar
½ teaspoon coarsely ground
    black pepper
½ teaspoon ground cumin
½ teaspoon chili powder
1 (15-ounce) can black beans,
    drained and rinsed
2 ears Chipotle Grilled Corn
    (page 137)

1. Whisk together the first 8 ingredients in a medium bowl. Add the black beans, tossing to coat.

2. Cut the kernels from cobs; discard cobs. Add the kernels to the salad, tossing to coat.

BLACK BEANS AND RICE

As a hearty vegetarian meal or a sublime side dish, black beans and rice are a Tex-Mex staple.

Hands-on: 15 minutes ★ **Total: 45 minutes** ★ **Serves 8**

1½ cups uncooked long-grain rice
3 (15-ounce) cans black beans
1 cup chopped onion
1 cup chopped green bell pepper
3 garlic cloves, minced
2 teaspoons olive oil
1 (14-ounce) can chicken broth
1 (6-ounce) can tomato paste
1 teaspoon ground cumin

¾ teaspoon dried crushed red pepper
Toppings: shredded Cheddar cheese, sliced radishes, chopped tomatoes, chopped fresh cilantro, sliced green onions, sliced jalapeño peppers

1. Prepare rice according to package directions.

2. Meanwhile, drain and rinse 2 cans black beans. (Do not drain remaining can of black beans.)

3. Sauté onion, bell pepper, and garlic in hot oil in a Dutch oven over medium-high 5 minutes or until tender. Stir in drained and undrained beans, chicken broth, tomato paste, cumin, and dried crushed red pepper. Bring to a boil; reduce heat, and simmer, stirring occasionally, 30 minutes. Add salt to taste. Serve with hot cooked rice and desired toppings.

KENTUCKY WONDER BEANS

What could a Kentucky bean be doing in a cookbook all about Texas? Believe it or not, this leggy heirloom bean was originally introduced under the name Texas Pole, as recorded in an 1864 issue of The Country Gentleman, *but the name changed to Kentucky Wonder in 1877. Whatever you want to call them, these beans served with crisp, smoky bacon and a hefty twist of freshly ground black pepper are truly wonderful.*

Hands-on 30 minutes ★ **Total** 2 hours, 30 minutes ★ **Serves** 6 to 8

8 bacon slices
1 medium onion, thinly sliced
4 garlic cloves, minced
1 bay leaf
2 fresh thyme sprigs
2 pounds fresh green beans
   (such as Kentucky Wonders),
   trimmed

1 teaspoon table salt
1 teaspoon freshly ground
   black pepper
¼ teaspoon dried crushed red
   pepper (optional)
1 cup chicken broth
2 tablespoons apple cider vinegar

1. Cook the bacon in a large Dutch oven over medium-low 8 minutes or until crisp; remove bacon, and drain on paper towels, reserving 2 tablespoons drippings in Dutch oven and 1 tablespoon drippings in a small bowl. Crumble the bacon.

2. Increase heat to medium-high. Sauté the onion, garlic, bay leaf, and thyme in hot drippings in Dutch oven 5 minutes or until onion is tender.

3. Stir in the beans, salt, black pepper, and, if desired, crushed red pepper. Add the broth and reserved 1 tablespoon bacon drippings, and bring to a boil. Cover, reduce heat, and simmer, stirring occasionally, 2 hours to 2 hours and 15 minutes or until beans are tender.

4. Remove from heat, and discard the bay leaf and thyme. Stir in the vinegar and crumbled bacon. Serve warm or at room temperature.

LA BARBECUE CHARRO BEANS

This hearty side is the closest you're going to get to genuine cowboy fare. By cowboys we mean los charros, the dashing gentleman horsemen of Mexico whose flashy equestrian skills captured the imaginations of generations. The kaleidoscope of flavors from layered spices and vibrant herbs distinguishes charro beans from less-than-authentic recipes for "cowboy beans" made with canned beans and ketchup.

Hands-on 20 minutes ★ **Total** 5 hours, 20 minutes, plus soaking time ★ **Serves** 8 to 10

1 (16-ounce) package dried pinto beans
1 yellow onion, chopped
½ cup canned crushed tomatoes
1 jalapeño pepper, seeded and chopped
¾ pound salt pork
1 tablespoon chili powder
2 teaspoons ground cumin
1½ teaspoons freshly ground black pepper
1 teaspoon garlic powder
½ cup chopped fresh cilantro

1. Place the pinto beans in a Dutch oven. Cover with cold water 2 inches above beans; cover and let soak 8 hours.

2. Drain the beans; transfer to a Dutch oven. Add the onion, next 7 ingredients, and water to cover 1½ inches above beans. Bring to a boil; cover, reduce heat, and simmer 1 hour, stirring occasionally. Partially uncover pot, and simmer 2½ hours.

3. Remove lid, and simmer 1 hour, stirring occasionally. Stir in the cilantro, and simmer 20 to 30 minutes or until beans are tender.

★ ★ ★
LONE STAR LEGENDS

La Barbecue

Austin

◇◇◇◇◇◇◇◇◇

La Barbecue is an unassuming food truck in Austin's Aztec Food Park next to neighborhood dive bar Stay Gold and Leal's Tire Shop. Though renowned for their brisket (for the record, La Barbecue has received kudos from the likes of the *Condé Nast Traveler* and *TIME* magazine), their delicious side dishes are worthy of recognition. These charro beans are a popular item in both BBQ and Tex-Mex Cuisine.

1906 E. Cesar Chavez St
Austin, TX 78702
512-605-9696
labarbecue.com

POTATO SALAD WITH SWEET PICKLES

Potato salad is adored throughout the South, but no two recipes are exactly the same. In Central Texas, picnickers enjoy their spuds with onion, dill, and mayonnaise or German-style with a vinegar or mustard base alongside traditional Deutschland fare.

Hands-on 20 minutes ★ **Total** 1 hour ★ **Serves** 8 to 10

1 (4-pound) bag large baking potatoes
2½ teaspoons table salt
1 cup mayonnaise
1 tablespoon spicy brown mustard
¾ teaspoon ground black pepper
3 hard-cooked eggs, grated
½ cup chopped celery
⅓ cup sweet salad cube pickles
Garnish: chopped fresh parsley

1. Cook the potatoes in boiling water to cover and salted with 1 teaspoon of the salt for 40 minutes or until tender; drain and cool 10 to 15 minutes.

2. Stir together the mayonnaise, mustard, pepper, and remaining 1½ teaspoons salt in a large bowl.

3. Peel the potatoes, and cut into 1-inch cubes. Add the warm potato cubes, grated eggs, celery, and pickles to bowl, and gently toss with the mayonnaise mixture. Serve immediately, or, if desired, cover and chill.

GRILLED ROMAINE CAESAR SALAD

Grilled romaine lettuce is a smoky and satiating take on the typical chilled Caesar salad. The creamy dressing and Garlic-Thyme Croutons balance the dense notes of the char from grilling.

Hands-on 20 minutes ★ **Total** 20 minutes ★ **Serves** 6

GARLIC-THYME CROUTONS

¼ cup olive oil

2 garlic cloves, pressed

2 teaspoons chopped fresh thyme

8 ounces crusty French bread, cut into ½-inch cubes

SALAD

½ cup freshly grated Parmesan cheese

¼ cup fresh lemon juice

2 tablespoons mayonnaise

1 teaspoon Dijon mustard

4 garlic cloves

½ cup olive oil

3 romaine lettuce hearts, halved lengthwise

Shaved Parmesan cheese

1. Make the Garlic-Thyme Croutons: Heat the oil in a large skillet over medium. Add the garlic; cook 30 seconds. Add the thyme, bread cubes, and table salt and black pepper to taste, tossing well to coat. Cook 5 minutes, stirring constantly, until bread is toasted. Remove croutons from pan to cool.

2. Make the Salad: Preheat the grill to 350° to 400°F (medium-high).

3. Combine the cheese, lemon juice, mayonnaise, Dijon mustard, and garlic in a food processor. Pulse until combined. With food processor running, slowly add ⅓ cup of the oil, and process until smooth.

4. Brush the romaine hearts with remaining oil. Grill the romaine hearts, cut sides down, 2 to 3 minutes or until charred.

5. Place 1 romaine heart on each plate. Drizzle with the dressing, and sprinkle with croutons and shaved Parmesan.

FRESH OKRA AND TOMATOES

This fresh and simple side is a descendant of a long line of okra-and-tomato dishes perfected by Creole chefs who picked up recipes from their parents or grandparents. Cooking the okra for a fairly short amount of time allows all the flavors to sing together and helps to prevent the okra from becoming slimy.

Hands-on 35 minutes ★ **Total** 35 minutes ★ **Serves** 4 to 6

1 small onion, chopped
2 tablespoons olive oil
2 garlic cloves, minced
1 pound fresh okra, sliced
½ teaspoon table salt
5 large plum tomatoes, diced
2 teaspoons Creole seasoning
Hot sauce (optional)

Sauté the onion in hot oil in a large skillet over medium 5 to 6 minutes or until tender and beginning to brown. Add the garlic, and sauté 1 minute. Add the okra and salt, and cook 3 minutes or until okra begins to soften. Stir in the tomatoes and Creole seasoning, and cook 5 minutes or until okra is tender. Add salt and freshly ground black pepper to taste and, if desired, hot sauce.

Note: We tested with Tony Chachere's Creole Seasoning.

★ ★ ★
BEYOND BBQ

Okra

Okra was carried to America in the pockets of African slaves working Southern plantations. The nourishing vegetable was scrumptious to eat by itself or in soup, and white plantation owners soon learned to love the delicate "lady's fingers" as well. The people who knew okra best, however, also revered the healing properties of the vegetable. In *The Federal Writers' Project: Slave Narrative Project, Vol. 16,* Mary Kindred, a former slave on the Luke Hadnot Plantation in Jasper, Texas, recalled how the energizing properties of okra's small white seeds were invoked when coffee was rationed during the Civil War.

GRILLED SWEET POTATO PLANKS

Proof that you can indeed grill anything and everything, the potato's naturally sweet flavors are reinforced by a little charring in this homage to Native American cooking.

Hands-on 20 minutes ★ **Total** 20 minutes ★ **Serves 6**

⅓ cup olive oil
1 tablespoon minced shallot
1 tablespoon chopped fresh
   rosemary
1 teaspoon kosher salt

1 teaspoon coarsely ground
   black pepper
3 large sweet potatoes, peeled
   and cut into ¼-inch-thick slices
½ cup crumbled blue cheese

1. Preheat the grill to 350° to 400°F (medium-high). Stir together the first 5 ingredients in a small bowl. Brush the olive oil mixture over sweet potato slices.

2. Grill, covered with grill lid, 3 to 4 minutes on each side or until tender. Place the potatoes on a serving platter; sprinkle with blue cheese.

GREEN RICE

Arroz verde is a tasty and colorful spin on traditional Mexican baked rice.

Hands-on 18 minutes ★ **Total** 48 minutes ★ **Makes 4¼ cups**

1 tablespoon butter
1 medium onion, quartered
4 garlic cloves, crushed
1 cup uncooked long-grain rice
1 cup loosely packed fresh
   cilantro

2 poblano peppers, stemmed
   and seeded
1¾ cups chicken broth
¾ teaspoon table salt

1. Preheat the oven to 350°F. Melt the butter in a 3-quart ovenproof saucepan over medium-high; add the onion and garlic. Sauté 4 minutes or until tender, making sure onion wedges remain intact. Remove the onion and garlic from the saucepan. Add the rice to pan; cook, stirring constantly, 2 minutes or until golden brown.

2. Process the cilantro, poblano peppers, and 1 cup of the chicken broth in a blender until smooth. Add the cilantro mixture, remaining ¾ cup of the chicken broth, and salt to saucepan; stir to combine.

3. Bake, covered, at 350°F for 25 minutes or until liquid is absorbed and rice is tender. Remove from oven, and let stand, covered, 5 minutes.

CHEESE GRITS AND ROASTED TOMATOES

Grits form the base to so many Southern dishes. Loaded with juicy roasted tomatoes, this cheesy side pairs well with Caribbean Shrimp Kabobs (page 121).

Hands-on 30 minutes ★ **Total** 1 hour, including tomatoes ★ **Serves** 4

½ cup heavy cream
2 tablespoons unsalted butter
2 teaspoons kosher salt
3 cups water
1 cup uncooked stone-ground
    yellow grits

2 ounces cream cheese
¼ cup finely grated extra-sharp
    Cheddar cheese
Roasted Tomatoes (recipe below)
Garnish: fresh chives

1. Bring the first 3 ingredients and 3 cups water to a boil in a medium saucepan over medium-high. Stir in the grits, and reduce heat to medium-low. Cover and simmer, stirring occasionally, 15 to 20 minutes or until tender.

2. Fold in the cheeses, stirring until melted; remove from heat. Cover and let stand 5 minutes. Transfer to a serving platter. Top with the Roasted Tomatoes.

ROASTED TOMATOES

Make a double batch of Roasted Tomatoes, and pair the juicy gems with a cheese tray, salad, or grilled meat.

Hands-on 5 minutes ★ **Total** 33 minutes ★ **Makes** 1½ cups

1 pound halved cherry tomatoes
1 tablespoon extra virgin olive oil
1 tablespoon red wine vinegar
1 teaspoon honey

¼ teaspoon kosher salt
¼ teaspoon freshly ground
    black pepper

Preheat the oven to 400°F. Toss together the cherry tomatoes, olive oil, vinegar, honey, salt, and pepper in a baking dish. Let stand 10 minutes. Bake at 400°F for 18 minutes or until tender.

Pappa Charlies Barbeque

Houston

◇◇◇◇◇◇◇◇◇

A brick-and-mortar restaurant in EaDo (East Downtown Houston) was a change of pace from the 20-foot food trailer and competition barbecue team led by Wesley Jurena. Established in 2009, Pappa Charlies is a start-up rapidly earning respect in the barbecue scene with every serving of peppery pork ribs, bacon-wrapped smoked meatloaf, and loaded macaroni and cheese creations that come topped with boudin, brisket, or chicken. The positive reviews from locals and the recent host of foodie award nominations don't hurt business either.

2012 Rusk St
Houston, TX 77003
(832) 940-1719
pappacharliesbbq.com

CLASSIC BAKED MACARONI AND CHEESE

Freshly grated Cheddar cheese lends a creamier texture to homemade baked macaroni and cheese, making it a constant crowd-pleaser.

Hands-on 27 minutes ★ **Total** 47 minutes ★ **Serves** 6 to 8

2 cups milk
2 tablespoons butter
2 tablespoons all-purpose flour
½ teaspoon table salt
¼ teaspoon freshly ground black pepper

1 (10-ounce) block extra-sharp Cheddar cheese, shredded
¼ teaspoon ground red pepper (optional)
½ (16-ounce) package elbow macaroni, cooked

1. Preheat the oven to 400°F. Lightly grease a 2-quart baking dish. Microwave the milk at HIGH 1½ minutes. Melt the butter in a large skillet or Dutch oven over medium-low; whisk in flour until smooth. Cook, whisking constantly, 1 minute.

2. Gradually whisk in the warm milk, and cook, whisking constantly, 5 minutes or until thickened.

3. Whisk in the salt, black pepper, 1 cup of the shredded cheese, and, if desired, red pepper until smooth; stir in the pasta. Spoon the pasta mixture into prepared baking dish; top with remaining cheese. Bake at 400°F for 20 minutes or until golden and bubbly.

HOME-STYLE HUSH PUPPIES

These tiny fritters are packed with flavor thanks to freshly chopped green onions, ground red pepper, and paprika. Frying them, and watching carefully, ensures maximum outer crispiness and inner tenderness.

Hands-on 20 minutes ★ **Total** 30 minutes ★ **Serves** 6 to 8

Vegetable oil
¾ cup plain yellow cornmeal
½ cup (2.13 ounces) all-purpose flour
1 tablespoon baking powder
1 tablespoon sugar
1 teaspoon baking soda
1 teaspoon table salt

½ teaspoon garlic powder
¼ teaspoon paprika
¼ teaspoon ground red pepper
¾ cup buttermilk
1 large egg, lightly beaten
¼ cup chopped green onions
Tartar sauce

1. Pour the oil to a depth of 2 inches into a Dutch oven; heat to 350°F. Combine the cornmeal and next 8 ingredients in a large bowl. Add the buttermilk, egg, and green onions; stir just until moistened. Let stand 10 minutes (batter will be fluffy).

2. Drop the batter by rounded tablespoonfuls into hot oil, and fry, in batches, 2 to 3 minutes on each side or until golden. Drain on a wire rack over paper towels. Serve immediately with tartar sauce.

SKILLET CORNBREAD

If a cast-iron skillet isn't close at hand, cook this sweet cornbread in muffin tins or a cake pan.

Hands-on 10 minutes ★ **Total** 35 minutes ★ **Serves** 10 to 12

1¼ cups finely ground stone-
    ground yellow cornmeal
¾ cup (3.19 ounces) all-purpose flour
1 teaspoon baking soda
1 teaspoon baking powder
1 teaspoon table salt

¾ cup frozen whole kernel
    corn, thawed
1¼ cups buttermilk
⅓ cup vegetable or canola oil
2 tablespoons honey
2 large eggs

1. Preheat the oven to 400°F. Heat a 10-inch cast-iron skillet in the oven 5 minutes.

2. Stir together the cornmeal and next 4 ingredients in a large bowl; stir in the corn. Whisk together the buttermilk and next 3 ingredients; add to the cornmeal mixture, stirring just until dry ingredients are moistened. Pour the batter into hot greased skillet.

3. Bake at 400°F for 25 to 30 minutes or until golden brown and a wooden pick inserted in center comes out clean.

PEACH-CHILE ICE POPS

These homemade frozen pops are a refreshing—but never boring—summer treat.

Hands-on 20 minutes ★ **Total** 8 hours, 35 minutes ★
Makes 10 frozen pops

⅔ cup sugar
1 tablespoon light corn syrup
¼ teaspoon table salt
3 tablespoons water
2 (¼-inch-thick) jalapeño
   pepper slices (with seeds)
4 large peaches, peeled
   and quartered

1½ teaspoons firmly packed
   lime zest
¼ cup fresh lime juice
10 food-safe wooden craft
   sticks

1. Bring the first 3 ingredients and 3 tablespoons water to a boil in a small saucepan over medium. Boil, stirring constantly, 1 to 2 minutes or just until sugar dissolves. Add the pepper slices, and cook, stirring occasionally, 1 minute. Remove from heat; let stand 15 minutes. Discard the jalapeño pepper slices.

2. Process the sugar syrup, peaches, and next 2 ingredients in a food processor until smooth, stopping to scrape down sides as needed. Pour the mixture into 10 (2-ounce) plastic pop molds. Top with lids of pop molds, and freeze 1 hour. Insert craft sticks, leaving 1½ to 2 inches sticking out, and freeze 7 more hours or until sticks are solidly anchored and pops are completely frozen.

★ ★ ★
BEYOND BBQ

Dueling Peach Capitals

The fertile knolls of Texas Hill Country are replete with farm stands and pick-your-own orchards selling juicy peaches. Pride for the fruit is so robust that two places in the region claim to be the Peach Capital of Texas. Peaches have flourished in Parker County since the J.K. Johnson family planted acres of peach trees and revamped pruning techniques in 1938. In 1991 the state legislature named Parker County the official peach capital of Texas. Some 200 miles south is Stonewall, another prolific peach producer. Since the 1960s Stonewall has celebrated the blushing fruit with its Peach JAMboree and Rodeo. To locals, Stonewall is the true birthplace of Hill Country peach farming and unofficially bears the title of Peach Capital of Texas, thanks to German settlers who first cultivated the fruit.

ORCHARD PEACH CRISP

When the peaches ripen during high summer in the Texas Hill Country, the most decadent pies, cobblers, and crisps also appear. Crisps, unlike pies and cobblers, are more rustic and less fussy to prepare, making them an easy dessert favorite.

Hands-on 15 minutes ★ **Total** 1 hour, 30 minutes ★ **Serves** 8 to 10

8 cups sliced peeled ripe peaches
½ cup granulated sugar
1½ tablespoons cornstarch
1 tablespoon fresh lemon juice
1 cup firmly packed brown sugar

1 cup (4.25 ounces) all-purpose flour
4 ounces (½ cup) cold butter, cut into pieces
1 cup uncooked regular oats

1. Preheat the oven to 375°F. Lightly grease a 13- x 9-inch baking dish. Combine the first 4 ingredients in a large bowl until peaches are well coated. Pour the mixture into prepared baking dish.

2. Combine the brown sugar and flour in a large bowl; cut in the butter with a fork or pastry blender until mixture is crumbly; stir in the oats. Sprinkle over the peach mixture.

3. Bake at 375°F for 1 hour and 5 minutes to 1 hour and 10 minutes or until the topping is golden brown and center is bubbly. Cool 10 minutes before serving.

SUMMER FRUIT COBBLER

Food historians have traced the modern fruit cobbler to the American Old West, where it was cooked in deep-dish skillets over open flames. Its name harkens back to when cowboy cooks had to "cobble" their dessert out of whatever was around at the moment, with irresistibly delectable results.

Hands-on: 20 minutes ★ **Total:** 1 hour, 25 minutes ★ **Serves** 6 to 8

3 tablespoons cornstarch
1½ cups sugar
3 cups coarsely chopped, peeled
    fresh nectarines
2 cups fresh blueberries
1 cup fresh raspberries
4 ounces (½ cup) butter, softened

2 large eggs
1½ cups (6.4 ounces) all-purpose
    flour
1½ teaspoons baking powder
1 (8-ounce) container sour cream
½ teaspoon baking soda

1. Preheat the oven to 350°F. Lightly grease an 11- x 7-inch baking dish. Stir together the cornstarch and ½ cup of the sugar. Toss the nectarines and berries with cornstarch mixture, and spoon into prepared baking dish.

2. Beat the butter at medium speed with an electric mixer until fluffy; gradually add remaining 1 cup sugar, beating well. Add the eggs, 1 at a time, beating just until blended after each addition.

3. Combine the flour and baking powder. Stir together the sour cream and baking soda. Add the flour mixture to butter mixture alternately with the sour cream mixture, beginning and ending with flour mixture. Beat at low speed just until blended after each addition. Spoon the batter over fruit mixture.

4. Bake at 350°F for 45 minutes; shield loosely with aluminum foil to prevent excessive browning; bake at 350°F for 20 to 25 more minutes or until a wooden pick inserted in center comes out clean.

Margarita Myth

Like most legendary heroes whose origin is recorded as a patchwork of rumors, the genesis of the margarita is just as shrouded in mystery and controversy. One thing that is clear, however, is the cocktail's strong tie to Texas. Some mixologists believe the creation can be credited to a young Dallas socialite named Margarita Sames. While hosting a Christmas party in 1948 with friends in Acapulco, Margarita mixed one part Cointreau, three parts tequila, and one part lime juice garnished with a rim of coarse salt. Margarita's influential friends in attendance included Conrad Nicholson Hilton, founder of Hilton Hotels; Joseph Drown, owner of the Hotel Bel-Air; and Shelton McHenry, owner of the nightclub Tail o' the Cock in Beverly Hills, all of whom she credited with helping popularize the beverage.

TEQUILA LIME PIE

Tequila, the distilled nectar of the blue agave plant, mixed with lime make this pie reminiscent of a margarita—and a potent addition to any gathering.

Hands-on 15 minutes ★ **Total** 2 hours, 40 minutes, plus chilling time ★ **Serves** 10 to 12

1½ cups graham cracker crumbs
5 tablespoons (⅓ cup) butter, melted
¼ cup firmly packed light brown sugar
3 (14-ounce) cans sweetened condensed milk

5 large egg yolks
1 cup fresh Key lime juice (about 2 pounds Key limes)*
½ cup tequila
Garnishes: sweetened whipped cream, lime slices

1. Preheat the oven to 350°F. Stir together the first 3 ingredients; firmly press mixture on the bottom and up sides of a 9- or 10-inch deep-dish pie plate.

2. Whisk together the condensed milk and egg yolks in a large bowl until blended. Gradually whisk in the lime juice and tequila until well blended. Pour the mixture into the prepared crust.

3. Bake at 350°F for 25 minutes or until set around edges. (Pie will be slightly jiggly.) Cool completely on a wire rack (about 2 hours). Cover and chill 8 hours.

Regular lime juice may be substituted for Key lime juice.

TEXAS PECAN PIE

A Texas Thanksgiving or Christmas is incomplete without pecan pie. The pecan, Texas' state nut, is presented in all its glory when nestled inside a lovingly crafted crust.

Hands-on 15 minutes ★ **Total** 4 hours, not including pie dough ★ **Serves** 8 to 10

Piecrust (recipe below)
¾ cup firmly packed brown sugar
¾ cup light corn syrup
2 ounces (¼ cup) butter, melted
1 teaspoon white vinegar

1 teaspoon vanilla extract
¼ teaspoon table salt
3 large eggs, lightly beaten
1¼ cups pecan halves

1. Preheat the oven to 425°F. Prepare the Piecrust. Roll out the dough into a 12-inch circle on a lightly floured surface. Place in a 9-inch pie plate; fold edges under, and crimp. Line the dough with aluminum foil; fill with pie weights or dried beans.

2. Bake at 425°F for 15 minutes or until the crust is set. Remove pie weights and foil; bake at 425°F for 10 more minutes or until the crust is lightly golden. Cool on a wire rack 30 minutes.

3. Reduce oven temperature to 350°F. Whisk together the brown sugar and next 6 ingredients. Pour into the cooled crust. Arrange the pecans on top of filling.

4. Bake at 350°F for 45 to 50 minutes or until golden brown and center is almost set, shielding edges with foil during last 15 minutes of baking to prevent excessive browning, if necessary. Cool completely on a wire rack (about 2 hours).

PIECRUST

Hands-on 10 minutes ★ **Total** 1 hour, 35 minutes, including chilling time ★ **Makes** 1 (9-inch) crust

1¼ cups (5.3 ounces) all-purpose
  flour
Pinch of table salt

4 ounces (½ cup) cold unsalted
  butter, cubed
¼ cup ice water

1. Pulse the flour and salt in a food processor 3 or 4 times. Add the butter; pulse 5 or 6 times or until crumbly. With processor running, gradually add the ice water until the dough forms a ball and pulls away from the sides of bowl. Add more ice water if necessary. Shape the dough into a flat disk. Wrap in plastic wrap, and chill 30 minutes.

2. Preheat the oven to 425°F. Roll the dough into a 12-inch circle on a lightly floured surface. Fit into a 9-inch pie plate; crimp the edges. Line the dough with aluminum foil, and fill with pie weights or dried beans.

3. Bake at 425°F for 15 minutes. Remove weights and foil, and bake at 425°F for 10 more minutes or until lightly browned. Transfer to a wire rack, and cool completely.

PECAN PIE BARS

Traditional pecan pie takes a turn as bite-size bars perfect for holiday gifting and midnight snacking and that can easily be made ahead. Make sure the butter is cold when you blend it into the flour. The crust will bake up to crispy perfection.

Hands-on 15 minutes ★ **Total** 2 hours, 55 minutes ★
Serves 36

3 cups (12.8 ounces)
   all-purpose flour
1 cup granulated sugar
¼ teaspoon table salt
6 ounces (¾ cup) cold butter,
   cut up
1½ cups light corn syrup

1 cup firmly packed light
   brown sugar
2 ounces (¼ cup) butter
4 large eggs, lightly beaten
2½ cups coarsely chopped
   pecans
1 teaspoon vanilla extract

1. Preheat the oven to 350°F. Grease a 15- x 10-inch jelly-roll pan. Whisk together the flour, granulated sugar, and salt in a large bowl. Cut the cold butter into the flour mixture with a pastry blender or fork until crumbly. Press the mixture into the bottom of prepared jelly-roll pan. Bake at 350°F for 17 to 20 minutes or until edges are light golden brown.

2. Combine the corn syrup, brown sugar, and ¼ cup butter in a medium saucepan; bring to a boil, whisking to dissolve sugar. Cool 5 minutes. Whisk the eggs in a large bowl. Gradually whisk half of the hot syrup mixture into the eggs; gradually whisk the egg mixture into remaining hot syrup mixture, whisking constantly. Stir in the pecans and vanilla. Spread the pecan mixture over the crust. Bake at 350°F for 20 minutes or until set. Cool completely on a wire rack (about 2 hours). Cut into 36 squares.

★ ★ ★
BEYOND BBQ

Texas State Tree

Georgia may be the biggest producer of pecans in the U.S., but this distinctive nut was discovered by Spanish explorers as they moved from Mexico into Texas. Many of the native Texas tribes that lived along the coast, including the Karankawa and the Coahuiltecans, feasted on Central Texas pecans along the riverbanks in the fall. In 1919, the humble pecan tree was recognized as the state tree of Texas.

COCONUT FLAN

The tropical notes of coconut pair perfectly with the slightly burnt flavor of the sugar that caramelizes in the bottom of the pan as this dessert cooks. Now globally popular, creamy, custardy flan was most likely brought to Texas from Spanish settlers in Mexico.

Hands-on 25 minutes ★ **Total** 6 hours, 40 minutes ★ **Serves** 8

1 cup sugar
½ cup water
1 (13.66-ounce) can coconut milk
1 cup cream of coconut

1 cup sweetened condensed milk
1 teaspoon vanilla extract
5 large eggs
Garnish: toasted coconut flakes

1. Preheat the oven to 325°F. Lightly grease 8 (6-ounce) ramekins. Combine the sugar and ½ cup water in a heavy saucepan; cook over low 10 to 12 minutes or until sugar melts and turns a light golden brown. Remove from heat; immediately pour the hot caramelized sugar into prepared ramekins. Let stand 6 minutes or until the sugar hardens.

2. Whisk together the coconut milk and next 4 ingredients in a large bowl until smooth. Pour the mixture evenly over the sugar in each ramekin. Place ramekins in a large roasting pan. Add hot tap water to pan to a depth of 1 inch. Cover loosely with aluminum foil.

3. Bake at 325°F for 55 minutes to 1 hour and 10 minutes or until slightly set. (Flan will jiggle when pan is shaken.) Remove ramekins from water bath; place on a wire rack. Cool completely (about 1 hour). Cover and chill at least 4 hours. Run a knife around edges of flans to loosen; invert flans onto serving plates.

Blue Bonnet Cafe

Marble Falls

◇◇◇◇◇◇◇◇◇

When driving through the Hill Country town of Marble Falls, it's only fitting to make a stop at the Blue Bonnet Cafe. Since 1929, this roadside diner offers most of the customary cafe foods you'd expect, including burgers, patty melts, chicken-fried steak with cream gravy, and a long list of flattop grill breakfast fare. The best time to visit is weekdays between the hours of 3 p.m. and 5 p.m. for the daily Pie Happy Hour, which offers a slice of pie from 10 daily selections and a cup of coffee for three bucks.

---

211 US Highway 281
Marble Falls, TX 78654
830-693-2344
bluebonnetcafe.net

CINNAMON ICE CREAM

This heavenly ice-cream blend pulls inspiration from the distinctive flavors of horchata, a beverage served in Spain and Latin America. The delicious drink made with rice milk, vanilla, and cinnamon has made its way into the hearts of Tex-Mex fans. This ice cream treat is divine over a chocolate brownie, cobbler, or pie.

Hands-on 15 minutes ★ **Total** 6 hours, 45 minutes ★
Makes 3 cups

½ vanilla bean
1¾ cups milk
½ cup sugar

4 large egg yolks
¼ teaspoon ground cinnamon

1. Split the vanilla bean lengthwise, and scrape out seeds. Cook the milk, vanilla bean, and seeds in a heavy nonaluminum saucepan over medium, stirring often, 6 minutes or just until bubbles appear (do not boil); remove from heat.

2. Whisk together the sugar and egg yolks in a medium bowl until thick and pale. Gradually whisk in about ½ cup of the hot milk mixture into yolks. Add the yolk mixture to remaining hot milk mixture, whisking constantly. Cook over medium-low, whisking constantly, 2 minutes or until mixture thickens and coats a spoon. (Do not boil.) Remove from heat; pour through a fine wire-mesh strainer into a bowl. Whisk in the cinnamon, and let stand 30 minutes. Cover and chill 4 hours.

3. Pour mixture into the freezer container of a 1½-quart electric ice-cream maker, and freeze according to manufacturer's instructions. (Instructions and times may vary.)

BANANA PUDDING

To most Southerners, from the South Atlantic States to the West South-Central States, banana pudding tastes like homecoming. The key to nailing the nostalgic taste of this dessert is investing the time to curate a homemade pudding instead of using the shortcut of store-bought varieties.

Hands-on 25 minutes ★ **Total** 7 hours, 25 minutes ★ **Serves** 8 to 12

1 cup sugar
¼ cup cornstarch
1 teaspoon table salt
4 cups milk
4 large egg yolks, lightly beaten
2 tablespoons butter
1 teaspoon vanilla extract
¼ teaspoon almond extract (optional)

1½ (11-ounce) boxes vanilla wafers
4 to 5 ripe bananas, cut into ¼-inch slices
Sweetened whipped cream (optional)
Garnish: chopped vanilla wafers

1. Whisk together the first 3 ingredients in a medium-size heavy saucepan. Gradually whisk in the milk, whisking until well blended. Bring to a boil over medium, whisking constantly. Boil, whisking constantly, 2 minutes or until thickened. Remove pan from heat.

2. Whisk the egg yolks until slightly thick and pale. Gradually whisk about one-fourth of the hot milk mixture into the yolks. Add the yolk mixture to remaining hot milk mixture, whisking constantly. Bring the mixture to a light boil. Cook, whisking constantly, 1 minute. Remove from heat, and whisk in the butter, vanilla, and, if desired, almond extract.

3. Transfer the mixture to a shallow baking dish. Place plastic wrap directly on the cream mixture (to prevent a film from forming), and chill 3 to 4 hours.

4. Arrange one-third of the vanilla wafers in a single layer on bottom and sides of a 13- x 9-inch baking dish. Top with half of the banana slices and half of pudding. Repeat procedure with remaining wafers, banana slices, and pudding. Cover and chill 4 to 24 hours. Top with the whipped cream, if desired.

LEMON-LAVENDER POUND CAKE

The alkaline limestone soil found in the fertile Texas Hill Country is home to an impressive acreage of lavender fields that give Provence a run for its money. The soil composition is comparable to that of southeastern France and produces extensive lavender fields for botanic, cosmetic, and culinary uses. This family recipe was developed with Texas lavender fields in mind, and it's an excellent addition to a brunch or tea party.

Hands-on 20 minutes ★ **Total** 3 hours, 15 minutes ★ **Serves** 12 to 16

2 teaspoons dried lavender buds
2¾ cups sugar
8 ounces (1 cup) butter, softened
¼ cup lavender honey*
6 large eggs
2 teaspoons firmly packed
   lemon zest

1 teaspoon vanilla extract
3 cups (12.8 ounces)
   all-purpose flour
½ teaspoon table salt
¼ teaspoon baking soda
1 cup sour cream

1. Preheat the oven to 325°F. Pulse the lavender and 2 tablespoons of the sugar in a spice grinder until lavender is finely ground; transfer to a bowl. Stir in remaining sugar.

2. Beat the butter at medium speed with a heavy-duty electric stand mixer until creamy. Gradually add the lavender mixture and honey; beat at medium speed 3 to 5 minutes or until light and fluffy. Add the eggs, 1 at a time, beating just until blended after each addition. Stir in the lemon zest and vanilla.

3. Combine the flour, salt, and baking soda. Add the flour mixture to the butter mixture alternately with sour cream, beginning and ending with flour mixture. Beat at low speed just until blended after each addition. Pour the batter into a buttered and floured 10-inch Bundt pan.

4. Bake at 325°F for 1 hour and 15 minutes to 1 hour and 20 minutes or until a long wooden pick inserted in center comes out clean, shielding with aluminum foil after 45 to 50 minutes to prevent excessive browning. Cool in pan on a wire rack 10 minutes; remove cake from pan to wire rack, and cool completely (about 1½ hours).

Regular honey may be substituted for lavender honey.

TEXAS SHEET CAKE

Texas claimed the sheet cake as its own in the mid-1900s. This particular recipe pulls in another Texas culinary contribution, Dr Pepper, which hails from Waco in Central Texas.

Hands-on 20 minutes ★ **Total** 2 hours, including frosting ★ **Serves** 24

CAKE

1½ cups spicy cola soft drink
    (such as Dr Pepper)
1 cup vegetable or canola oil
½ cup unsweetened cocoa
2 cups (8.5 ounces) all-purpose flour
1 cup granulated sugar

1 cup firmly packed light brown sugar
1½ teaspoons baking soda
½ teaspoon table salt
½ cup buttermilk
2 large eggs, lightly beaten
2 teaspoons vanilla extract

FUDGE FROSTING

4 ounces (½ cup) butter
½ (4-ounce) unsweetened
    chocolate baking bar, chopped
3 tablespoons milk
3 tablespoons spicy cola soft drink
(such as Dr Pepper)

4 cups powdered sugar
1 teaspoon vanilla extract
1¼ cups chopped toasted pecans

1. Make the Cake: Preheat the oven to 350°F. Lightly grease a 17½- x 12½-inch jelly-roll pan. Bring the first 3 ingredients to a boil in a medium saucepan over medium-high, stirring often. Remove from heat.

2. Whisk together the flour and next 4 ingredients in a large bowl until blended; add warm soft drink mixture. Whisk in the buttermilk, eggs, and vanilla. Pour the batter into prepared pan.

3. Bake at 350°F for 18 to 22 minutes or until a wooden pick inserted in center comes out clean.

4. Make the Fudge Frosting: Heat the butter and chocolate in a medium saucepan over medium-low, stirring constantly until melted and smooth. Remove from heat, and whisk in the milk and soft drink until blended. Stir in the sugar and vanilla. Beat at medium speed with an electric mixer until smooth and sugar dissolves. Pour over the warm cake, spreading gently to edges. Sprinkle with the chopped pecans. Cool completely in pan (about 1 hour).

NEIMAN MARCUS CAKE

This rich dessert has the texture of a brownie with traditional German chocolate cake ingredients and a sweet cream cheese topping. Many know the legend of the famous Neiman Marcus cookie recipe that was once purchased for $250, but this recipe from the Texas flagship store seems to have flown under the radar.

Hands-on 20 minutes ★ **Total** 2 hours ★ **Serves** 6 to 8

1 (4-ounce) unsweetened chocolate baking bar, chopped
6 ounces (¾ cup) butter, cut into pieces
2 cups granulated sugar
4 large eggs
½ cup milk

2 teaspoons vanilla extract
2¼ cups (9.6 ounces) all-purpose flour
1 teaspoon baking soda
½ teaspoon table salt
1 (8-ounce) package cream cheese, softened
2 cups powdered sugar

1. Preheat the oven to 350°F. Grease a 13- x 9-inch baking pan. Microwave the chocolate and butter in a large microwave-safe bowl at HIGH 1½ to 2 minutes or until melted and smooth, stirring at 30-second intervals. Whisk in the granulated sugar. Add 2 of the eggs, 1 at a time, whisking just until blended after each addition. Whisk in the milk and 1 teaspoon of the vanilla.

2. Combine the flour, baking soda, and salt in a bowl. Gradually add the flour mixture to chocolate mixture, whisking until blended. Pour the batter into prepared pan. (Batter will be thick.)

3. Beat the cream cheese and remaining 1 teaspoon vanilla at medium speed with an electric mixer until creamy. Gradually add the powdered sugar, beating well. Add remaining 2 eggs, 1 at a time, beating just until yellow disappears after each addition. Pour the mixture over chocolate mixture, and spread evenly, being careful not to mix layers.

4. Bake at 350°F for 40 minutes or until a wooden pick inserted in center comes out with a few moist crumbs. Cool completely on a wire rack (about 1 hour).

METRIC EQUIVALENTS

The recipes that appear in this cookbook use the standard United States method for measuring liquid and dry or solid ingredients (teaspoons, tablespoons, and cups). The information in the following charts is provided to help cooks outside the U.S. successfully use these recipes. All equivalents are approximate.

Metric Equivalents for Different Types of Ingredients

A standard cup measure of a dry or solid ingredient will vary in weight depending on the type of ingredient. A standard cup of liquid is the same volume for any type of liquid. Use the following chart when converting standard cup measures to grams (weight) or milliliters (volume).

Standard Cup	Fine Powder (ex. flour)	Grain (ex. rice)	Granular (ex. sugar)	Liquid Solids (ex. butter)	Liquid (ex. milk)
1	140 g	150 g	190 g	200 g	240 ml
¾	105 g	113 g	143 g	150 g	180 ml
⅔	93 g	100 g	125 g	133 g	160 ml
½	70 g	75 g	95 g	100 g	120 ml
⅓	47 g	50 g	63 g	67 g	80 ml
¼	35 g	38 g	48 g	50 g	60 ml
⅛	18 g	19 g	24 g	25 g	30 ml

Useful Equivalents for Liquid Ingredients by Volume

¼ tsp					=	1 ml	
½ tsp					=	2 ml	
1 tsp					=	5 ml	
3 tsp	=	1 Tbsp		=	½ fl oz	=	15 ml	
		2 Tbsp	= ⅛ cup	=	1 fl oz	=	30 ml	
		4 Tbsp	= ¼ cup	=	2 fl oz	=	60 ml	
		5 ⅓ Tbsp	= ⅓ cup	=	3 fl oz	=	80 ml	
		8 Tbsp	= ½ cup	=	4 fl oz	=	120 ml	
		10 ⅔ Tbsp	= ⅔ cup	=	5 fl oz	=	160 ml	
		12 Tbsp	= ¾ cup	=	6 fl oz	=	180 ml	
		16 Tbsp	= 1 cup	=	8 fl oz	=	240 ml	
		1 pt	= 2 cups	=	16 fl oz	=	480 ml	
		1 qt	= 4 cups	=	32 fl oz	=	960 ml	
					33 fl oz	=	1000 ml	= 1 l

Useful Equivalents for Dry Ingredients by Weight

(To convert ounces to grams, multiply the number of ounces by 30.)

1 oz	=	1/16 lb	=	30 g
4 oz	=	¼ lb	=	120 g
8 oz	=	½ lb	=	240 g
12 oz	=	¾ lb	=	360 g
16 oz	=	1 lb	=	480 g

Useful Equivalents for Length

(To convert inches to centimeters, multiply the number of inches by 2.5.)

1 in			=	2.5 cm	
6 in	= ½ ft		=	15 cm	
12 in	= 1 ft		=	30 cm	
36 in	= 3 ft	= 1 yd	=	90 cm	
40 in			=	100 cm	= 1 m

Useful Equivalents for Cooking/Oven Temperatures

	Fahrenheit	Celsius	Gas Mark
Freeze Water	32° F	0° C	
Room Temperature	68° F	20° C	
Boil Water	212° F	100° C	
Bake	325° F	160° C	3
	350° F	180° C	4
	375° F	190° C	5
	400° F	200° C	6
	425° F	220° C	7
	450° F	230° C	8
Broil			Grill

INDEX

PHOTO CONTRIBUTORS

Simon Andrews, Iain Bagwell, bjdlzx/Getty, Marian Cooper Cairns, Robbie Caponetto,
Caroline M. Cunningham, Jennifer Davick, flas100/Getty, Ryann Ford, Heather Chadduck Hillegas,
homydesign/Getty, Paul Horsley, Hugnoi/Getty, JHJackson/Getty, Krafla/Getty, Ladung/Getty,
Alison Miksch, Ben Miller/Getty, Buffy Hargett Miller, Lydia Pursell, Retrovizor/Getty, Chris M. Rodgers,
Hector Manuel Sanchez, Tarzhanova/Getty, Elke Van de Velde/Getty, yomoyo/Getty